Getting to Grips with Gangs: A Resource Guide for Teachers, Parents, Young People and the Wider Community

Letise Sampson

ISBN:978-1-9160667-0-0

CONTENTS

Biography - Letise Sampson

Young people across the country are facing a very new threat. Alongside the social issues they must deal with from bullying, online grooming, discrimination and mental health, this new threat, one can argue, is one of the most dangerous. Ripping families apart, creating fear in the local community and generating a new culture of violence as an acceptable way of dealing with conflict resolution.

Fuelled by the new wave of social media, online videos and propagated through new sub-genres of Hip Hop music such as Grime, Trap and Drill music, gangs have become the silent plague devouring the lives of young people in the streets.

Youths as young as 13 are losing their lives, just by being in the wrong postcode at the wrong time; or through the poor choices of friendships and peer affiliations. This has created a vicious cycle of revenge.

The innocent youth are now stuck in a place of lose-lose choices to survive, to join a gang or face the vulnerability of collateral damage.

It grieves my heart to turn on the TV or read the latest bulletin and see another life lost through this callous act of gang violence. Having a son myself, I wonder is this the prospect he will be looking forward to?

Over the last few years, I have researched hundreds of incidents to see whether there's was a similarity or trend and, even more importantly, to see whether there was a solution.

Gang violence is a difficult area to talk about because of all the surrounding issues: bereavement, poverty, dysfunctional families, external influences, abuse, peer pressure and more.

My hope is that by working through this book, thinking about the issues and reading about others' experiences, people will begin to make the right choices. If this book can help parents and schools to change the future of one gang member, to help them to say no to gangs and to fulfil their destiny, it would have been worth writing it.

My Story

I grew up in the north-west London borough of Brent, in a predominantly African Caribbean area. Gangs, knives, drugs and crime were something of a norm in the area. We accepted it as a way of life and became totally desensitised to the problems.

Young people actually looked up to neighbourhood gangsters; the more violent the gangs were, the more respect and reputation they built which generated fear and created a psychological protection for them. These gangs were then honoured in the form of urban legend folk tales.

I'll admit that my neighbourhood wasn't one of the worst crime-infested neighbourhoods in London, especially when compared with the urban tales from Peckham, Brixton, Hackney and Tottenham. But it shared the common characteristics; young people were being groomed into a gang fast and the gangs were turning more and more ruthless.

As I became conscious of gang violence from my own personal experiences, detailed later in this book, I realised this was something that had always been around me. But I chose to ignore the reality because until you have been a victim or seen things first-hand it doesn't ever hit home.

Most of all I saw how gangs destroyed innocent families through collateral damage. I made a choice: that this was not how my story would be written. I knew I had to do something radical. At 18 I decided to apply for University. I knew I couldn't get away from the area, so I guessed doing three years at university would create escapism from the harsh reality of living in London as a teen.

Going to the University of Bedford, I thought to myself, 'I'm free,' only to find out that gangs existed even there. With lots of students coming from various inner cities in the UK, the night life of university created a gang utopia. Although not as extreme as stabbings, gang-related problems spilled into the campus.

Another turning point was someone losing their life over a gang beating outside the main campus. At that point, I realised the issue was to do with the gang mentality itself and not necessarily where you're from.

After university, needing a place to live, I came back into the area. I made a choice to work hard to save money to buy a place outside of London and create a new life.

Graduating in Internet and Business, I found myself with a job at Sony BMG as an online marketing assistant. After two years working with young people from different walks of life, my mind-set changed and I realised life was bigger than a postcode. At 23 years old I started a media business which became successful. I was able to buy a place outside London and create a new life for myself.

Ten years later, now I am in my 30s. I have several successful businesses in Fitness, Corporate Events and Education with thousands of clients. I feel blessed that I was strong enough to make positive choices to get me in this position.

However, we're now in 2018 and sadly youth gang culture has evolved into something even more violent with the drive for reputation the biggest factor.

Never before have quarrels stemming from the most minor things, like posting a negative comment on social media about another gang, put young people's lives and the lives of their families at stake.

So, what can be done about this? I escaped the violence and was able to start again through one simple concept: **CHOICE**.

What young people need is hope and a new sense of positive direction. To understand that life is bigger than the postcode they live in. They need to feel like they are not suspects but can be prospects. This is done through life coaching techniques for older children and awareness of the situation for young children.

One of the things my mother taught me was to never forget where I came from. 2020 Dreams and 2020 Rising was created to help other young people see their vision clearly and turn their dreams into reality through positive, life-changing programmes.

CHAPTER 1: Introduction

The emergence of youth/street gangs are a cause of concern across the whole of the UK, especially in our inner cities and larger urban areas. Gang culture is linked to a wide range of societal problems from drugs and drink to sexual abuse and gun and knife crime.

We should all be aware of the negative impact gangs have on the fabric of society and of the tell-tale signs that reveal when our students and children are involved with gangs.

We must all do what we can to prevent young people from falling prey to the influence of gangs and to stop those who have become entangled from being lost completely. Every young person rescued from a gang prevents that gang from growing more powerful.

There are many reasons why young people get involved with gangs. Some of them are more external in nature, for example their family members and friends might be involved with gangs, they may have grown up in poverty or there could be a strong gang presence in their local neighbourhood.

Other factors, especially in the reputation-craving youth gangs of today, will be more internal. Some young people are attracted by the perceived glamour of gang life, the chance of earning respect from their peers or the opportunity to obtain material possessions.

Once inside a gang, additional factors can keep them trapped. Mainly a sense of fear stemming from threats and coercion from other gang members, a lack of protection from rival gangs a sense of loyalty to the gang and a fear of being punished for bad behaviour. Dependency on drugs or alcohol are also a factor.

Disconnection from Society

Attraction to the gang way of life and the formation of bonds between gang members is accompanied by a corresponding weakening of the connection between gang members and the wider community beyond the gang.

Gang members often drift away from their former friends and family members and drop conventional goals such as achieving good results at school or pursuing a particular career path. They stop attending sports clubs, music studios or other constructive groups and the gang becomes increasingly the centre of their existence.

In terms of attitude and behaviour, the moral convictions of the past are gradually dropped or allowed to fade, and the gang member starts to engage in delinquent behaviour.

These destructive and criminal behaviours can dominate the conversation when it comes to gangs and lead to a narrow focus on suppression measures such as gang sweeps and the like. This can take attention away from the equally important question of what it is about their lives that drives some young people into the gangs' clutches while their peers seem immune.

What are they missing from their lives and how do they receive it from a gang? This can be a painful but necessary question for parents in particular to ponder.

Youth gang members sometimes talk about the voice of the 'olders' being louder than that of their families. Did their child receive enough unconditional love and acceptance during their upbringing? Were they given clear boundaries? Did they have role models to look up to? Was their home environment happy and nurturing? Were they taught about the dangers of carrying knives?

Most young people want to do the right thing and fit into society as well-adjusted citizens. But conflicted by inner doubts and fears and scarred by experiences teenagers should never have to face they become at risk of losing their way. It can be a difficult task to steer them away from gangs and keep them on the straight and narrow.

Although gang members regularly display similar antisocial behaviours to one another, a 'one size fits all' solution is unlikely to work.

What we really need is a multi-pronged approach aimed at achieving long-term results with parents in particular, schools, community leader, police and other agents working together towards a common aim.

UK Gang Statistics

To get an idea of the scale of the problem we face, here are some gang-related statistics:

- In the first three months of 2019, 17 young people have been stabbed to death in London.
- By 21st May 2018, 25 young people had already been stabbed to death in London since the start of the year.
- There were 6,696 gun offences in England and Wales in 2017.
- Around half of all gun crime in the UK is gang-related.
- There were 36,998 knife offences in England and Wales in 2017.
- Around 20 per cent of all knife crime in the UK is gang-related.
- The Metropolitan Police have around 3,500 people on their controversial Gang Matrix.

*For more on knife crime, see my book: 'Getting Real with Guns and Knives'

How to Use This Book

This book is a 2020 Dreams publication created in partnership with 2020 Rising. 2020 Dreams provide high quality workshops on a wide range of topical young people's issues. More details on these are at the end of this book or at www.2020dreams.org.uk.

2020 Rising tackles those tough issues – like youth gangs – that all of us find it difficult to talk about.

This book is designed to be accessible not only to teachers and community group members but also to parents and students themselves.

If you are not a big reader, there are plenty of case studies, discussion points and activities dotted throughout.

This book will provide you with everything you might want to know about what a gang is, how a gang operates and how we can work together as a community to combat their threat and bring back our young people.

For Teachers:

- Based on established and recent research and latest reports.
- Broken down into bite-sized chapters to help lesson planning.
- Can be read cover-to-cover or dipped into.
- 'Discuss This' panels for class discussion.
- 'Try This' panels for class activities.

For Parents:

- Real life case studies.
- 'Discuss This' panel for discussions at home.
- 'Try This' panel for family activities.
- Guidance for improving communication at home.

- Advice for working with other parents and the community.

For Young People:

- 'Discuss This' panels gives you things to talk about at school or with your family.
- 'Try This' panels include fun and useful activities for home and school.
- Advice to help you get out of a gang or to say no to joining one.

For the Wider Community:

- Based on established and recent research and latest reports.
- Builds awareness about gang culture.
- Practical advice for tackling gangs in your community.

You will find out about the gang mentality, including the 'Three R's' (reputation, respect and retaliation) which are of major importance to how gangs operate, especially in 2018.

You can read about the grooming and initiation process and find out what a typical gang member looks like – and where they come from.

There are also sections on gang behaviour, female sexual exploitation, gang fashion, knife crime, mental health issues and drugs.

Importantly, this book shows how we can work together to deal effectively with gangs. We look at how to assess the level of gang activity in your neighbourhood and how to understand the negative effects that gangs have on our communities. We also explore various types of intervention.

You will learn about the different roles that the police and justice system, community organisations, schools and parents can play in tackling gang influence from Joint Enterprise convictions and suppression tactics to early family intervention and social approaches.

CHAPTER 2: Definition of A Gang

We might think we know what a gang is, but can we honestly define how a gang differs from a group of young friends hanging around a shopping centre or performing grime or trap music together? Even if those outside of a gang can come to an agreement as to what makes one, this doesn't mean that the individuals involved relate to that label.

Under questioning, a young person may deny being affiliated to a gang at all and insist that his or her fellow gang members are just friends. Other terms they might use are 'family,' 'breddrin' (brethren), 'crews,' 'cuz' (cousins) or 'my boys.'

This distinction matters because the way we define gangs has big implications for how young people are treated by the justice system. The same crime is likely to be treated more seriously if it is considered to be gang-related (you can read more about this in the next chapter and the chapter on Joint Enterprise).

The narrower and carefully considered a definition is, the more protection young people have from being unfairly labelled a gang member and having harsher sentences imposed. The more broader the definition, the more protection there is for citizens as the burden of proof is on the accused.

Here are some definitions of a gang taken from the UK and the US.

United Kingdom

The definition of a gang preferred by many UK bodies was drawn up in February 2009 by the Centre for Social Justice, a government think tank. In its 'Dying to Belong' report, this body defined a gang as:

A relatively durable, predominantly street-based group of young people who:

(1) see themselves (and are seen by others) as a discernible group,
(2) engage in a range of criminal activity and violence,
(3) identify with or lay claim over territory,
(4) have some form of identifying structural feature, and
(5) are in conflict with other, similar, gangs.

Bodies using this, or a similar definition, range include other government bodies (e.g. the Children's Commissioner who, in November 2017, wrote a report on the welfare of children in gangs) and local council safeguarding boards (LSCBs).

This definition is by no mean accepted across the board. However, it does remove the tendency for misbehaving youths to be automatically labelled as part of a gang.

This was something that the CSJ were keen to dispel in their 2009 report, which said: “The vast majority of groups of young people are not gangs, and the labelling of them as such can have negative consequences for all involved.”

Police and civilians should always keep this in mind before judging a group of youths. Alienating and punishing people for being in a group makes the problem worse!

United States

The federal definition of a gang, as taken from the Department of Justice and the Department of Homeland Security's Immigration and Customs Enforcement (ICE), is as follows:

An association of three or more individuals:

- ✓ Whose members collectively identify themselves by adopting a group identity which they use to create an atmosphere of fear or intimidation, frequently by employing one or more of the following: a common name, slogan, identifying sign, symbol, tattoo or other physical marking, style or colour of clothing, hairstyle, hand sign or graffiti;
- ✓ Whose purpose in part is to engage in criminal activity and which uses violence or intimidation to further its criminal objectives.
- ✓ Whose members engage in criminal activity or acts of juvenile delinquency that, if committed by an adult, would be crimes with the intent to enhance or preserve the association's power, reputation or economic resources.
- ✓ The definition goes on to say that the association may also possess some of the following characteristics:
- ✓ The members may employ rules for joining and operating within the association

- ✓ The members may meet on a recurring basis
- ✓ The association may provide physical protection of its members from others
- ✓ The association may seek to exercise control over a particular geographic location or region, or it may simply defend its perceived interests against rivals.
- ✓ The association may have an identifiable structure.

Activities: What is a Gang Anyway?

Discuss This!

What differences are there between how the UK and USA define gangs? Do these differences matter?

- ✓ What are the pros and cons of a narrow definition?
- ✓ What are the pros and cons of a broad definition?
- ✓ How would you feel if a friend who wasn't in a gang went to jail for a long time because the jury believed he or she was in a gang?
- ✓ How would your family feel it a gang member hurt you but got away with a short sentence because the jury didn't find enough evidence they were in a gang?

Try This!

1. Without looking at any examples, write a list of five things that define a gang.

2. Bring your answers back to your teacher or family and compare definitions.
3. What did you all agree on? Did you disagree on some things?

In the UK definition, unlike the US definition, there has to be evidence that members of a group see themselves as a gang. The US definitions of gang doesn't require this which gives more power to others (e.g. the police) to label young people as gang members.

This federal definition is modified in state definitions and the issue of defining gangs is a hot one there. For example, the state of Mississippi is currently engaged in what has been described as an escalating 'war on gangs' and there are cases whereby state prosecutors can increase sentences by five times or more if they can convince a jury that the offenders were part of a gang when they committed the offence (which could be as minor as selling 30 grams of cannabis).

To make their decision, police officers might draw upon the clothing and tattoos the defendants are wearing and under new proposed legislation (specifically Senate Bill 2868), it would be difficult for a judge to intervene unless they had solid reasons that to do so would serve the interests of justice.

Of course, with limited access to high quality legal defence, those from poor neighbourhoods would become worryingly dependent on the discretion of police officers.

The Mississippi bill comes hot on the heels of a similar broadening of gang definition in another southern state: Kentucky. House Bill 169 passed a House committee in February 2018 and, at the time of writing this book, was due to go before the full House for approval.

As well as defining gangs, this bill also punishes those, even children, who intentionally encourage or solicit another person to join a criminal gang. This is known as 'gang grooming'.

CHAPTER 3: Older Gang Members: Grooming and Initiation

The problem with gangs is that sometimes you may become affiliated with one without knowing. This brings me to the story of my good friend who was involved in gangs in Stratford and Stockwell.

He introduced me to a different world. Being in his late 20s, he was what you would call an 'older' and he looked at me as a potential mentee in the gang lifestyle. I was naive at the time and was happy that someone with a street credibility of his calibre would be willing to bring me into his crew.

Little did I know I was being groomed into becoming a gang member. It opened my eyes to a new world of constant near death experiences; just through my affiliation with him alone, I experienced at least six incidents of a threat to my life.

What is Grooming?

The process of grooming for gang membership is rarely covered in the mainstream media but grooming is featured a lot in an equally disturbing phenomenon: the grooming of children for sexual exploitation.

Gang grooming is the psychological process by which new gang members are recruited by older gang members. It often includes an initial period of encouragement, affection and attention and may be followed by violence and threats.

Children as young as 10 are being approached in the streets or even outside the school playground!

One tactic is to claim that the child is being targeted by a rival gang and to offer protection from harm. Other children and teenagers are drawn into gangs because they crave the attention and affection they are not receiving elsewhere or, like me, they look up to and respect an 'older.'

Initiation into Gang Life

I have mentioned the hierarchical structure of gangs earlier in the book. Another common part of the gang structure is the initiation process.

Once they have been drawn in through the grooming process, gang 'youngers' are often used as drug runners or for concealing weapons. This is because of the reduced risk of them being stopped and searched by police. They are also 'human shields,' protecting olders from being 'poked up' (i.e. stabbed) by rivals.

As they prove their worth, new gang members might be ordered to carry out criminal activities such as beatings, robbery, arson or vandalism.

The more violent the crime, the bigger their reputation and the higher their place in the gang hierarchy will be.

Coercing young people into carrying out acts of violence and antisocial behaviour has another effect. By moving from being a victim to a perpetrator of crime, the new recruits are even less likely to want to escape the gang for fear of being punished for their actions.

These are also 'rites of passage' which mark the movement from being on the outskirts of the gang to full membership (or from a child to an adult). In the language of the streets, a new gang member might be told they need to, 'show they're about that life.' If they successfully carry out the tasks given to them they will finally become 'certified' – i.e. a fully-fledged gang member.

Committing violent acts also reinforces the centrality of violence to the gang's existence and helps to further desensitise the individual to the violence that they will partake in and witness.

The physical pain and, sometimes, threat to life that the initiate suffers is outweighed by the emotional high that comes from having demonstrated courage and been accepted into a group. According to 'The Handbook of Gangs,' extreme initiation processes actually lead to closer bonding with a group than milder forms.

There are, of course, many urban myths around what happens within gang initiations and while there are undoubtedly some horrific rites out there, it is important to know that some have been made up and spread for shock factor.

After all, one way for a gang to gain notoriety and respect is by spreading sick tales of horrendous initiations which may never have actually occurred.

Once accepted by the group, the new gang member can expect to be rewarded with drugs, alcohol and material possessions such as clothes, jewellery, shoes or weapons. Perhaps most important of all, the gang member will feel a sense of belonging that they may never have experienced before.

Sexual exploitation is common within gangs with girls in particular at risk. As explained in a later chapter, girls are also enticed and accepted into the gang hierarchy through grooming and initiation.

Desistance: Leaving the Gang

Gang members often refer to the severe consequences gang members will face if they leave a gang. However, research involving ex-members suggests that this may be more a tool of intimidation than a real condition of gang desistance.

Nevertheless, the fear of consequences for leaving the gang combined with the real risk of being targeted by rival gang members or the authorities, can make it very difficult to help young people to disengage from gangs.

Well-meaning civilians should understand this when they talk about choice.

An Alternative Path to Acceptance

As a community, we clearly need to intervene earlier to prevent vulnerable young people from being lured into gang culture by older, manipulative gang members. However, we may also need to look at what young people are gaining from undergoing initiations because something is clearly speaking to them.

It seems that the initiation process is fulfilling a deep unmet need for respect and acceptance. Is it possible to provide an alternative route that is less destructive to society?

For example, in the book, 'Seven Pathways into and Out of Gangs' (from 'The Re-Evolution of American Street Gangs' collection), author Aaron Kipnis suggests taking inspiration from Boys to Men programmes and:

- ✓ Treating young people as they are, not how we want them to be.
- ✓ Being honest and direct but focusing on the positive.
- ✓ Being respectful (see the chapter on the 3 Rs!).
- ✓ Create joined-up services to form a safety net for those at risk.
- ✓ Recruit former gang members as leaders and programme designers.
- ✓ Provide opportunities for real economic advancement and inclusion in society.

There is no one easy solution to combat the powerful effects of grooming and gang initiation rituals but the more we can understand the psychology behind them, the more likely we can create effective interventions.

Activities: Know Your Enemy

Discuss This!

- ✓ Why do you think olders really want young teens to join their gang?
- ✓ Some olders admit that youngers are better for drugs running as they will be 'poked-up' instead of them. Would you take on that risk for an older?
- ✓ Some ex-gang members regret being involved in drugs because they kill people. How would you feel about drug running if someone you knew died because of drugs?
- ✓ How would your family feel if you got hurt and they couldn't bring anyone to justice?
- ✓ How would you feel if you found out someone else's child got hurt or killed because of a weapon you carried?

Try This!

Try this activity in pairs.
Imagine you have to get a package from A to B in the next five minutes (set a timer). In that time, come up with three ways to persuade them:

1. Bribery
2. Flattery
3. Threats (don't make it too violent)

The other person has to try and say 'no' to each attempt. Then swap over.
Which techniques do you think work best? What is the best way to say no?

CHAPTER 4: Peer-On-Peer & Online Grooming

Peer-on-peer grooming has been identified by some sources (e.g. Birmingham City Council) as a separate model of grooming from the standard gang initiation model.

This is because grooming does not always involve an older targeting a child or young teen. Peer-on-peer or near pear grooming is when young people (who are themselves already being groomed) draw their friends or other people of a similar age into gang culture.

Peer-on-Peer grooming affects girls as well as boys with girls used to entice their friends into a gang's network (in some cases to be sexually exploited).

The influence of peer-on-peer grooming is sometimes downplayed as was admitted by West Midlands Police in 2014 when they listed a lack of focus on peer-on-peer grooming as a failing in their investigations. Although the investigation wasn't looking into gang membership, the findings still highlight a potential blind spot that those working to tackle gangs need to keep in mind.

Peer-on-peer grooming is clearly going to be an effective tactic for gangs to employ since there will already be shared experiences and a sense of trust between peers.

Peer-on-peer gang grooming does not just happen in the street or outside of the school playground. Social media networks and chat applications are powerful channels by which gang members can exert their influence on peers. Unlike other forms of connection, social media and mobile phones enable 24 hour contact.

Online and Social Media Grooming

Back in 2013, The Birmingham Safeguarding Board highlighted the dangers of internet grooming, pointing out the fact that perpetrators could assume false identities and that online spaces weren't sufficiently monitored.

Vulnerable people, including those with emotional and mental health issues and learning disabilities, were deemed particularly at risk since the usual safeguards weren't in place online. The potential for children to be targeted maliciously via online apps has been highlighted recently with apps such as WhatsApp, Roblox and Sarahah attracting criticism for failing to do enough to police their users.

Via Online Channels, Gang Members Can:

Pretend to be a child to befriend them via chatrooms, social networks, email, SMS messaging, games and mobile apps. This helps them to gain trust that they would otherwise struggle to obtain.

- ✓ Contact targets while they are seemingly safe (at home or a friend's house).
- ✓ Stalk their victims and gain information about their day-to-day activities.
- ✓ Arrange to meet young people with intent of inducting them into a gang.

- ✓ Blackmail young people (particularly girls) by encouraging them to send sexualised images or videos.

The Characteristics of The Grooming Process

The basic grooming process can be divided into three stages: finding a target, grooming the target and initiation. This is similar to the 'grooming line' model designed by Barnardo's for victims of sexual exploitation.

With peer-on-peer grooming, the target is already in the groomer's social circle or immediate peer network, so the first stage is already completed. For older gang members, grooming might involve identifying a vulnerable child in a public place or online.

After starting a conversation, the gang member will obtain personal details such as the child's name, age and contact details.

Once a proper connection is established, grooming can start. Both positive actions (flattery, providing gifts, etc.) and negative ones (threats, intimidation, violence, etc.) may be used.

Even the apparently generous actions will eventually be used as a form of 'debt bondage,' with victims reminded that they owe the groomer for their presents.

The depths to which gang members will stoop to keep their target under close control should not be underestimated.

When threatening them with violence, for example, the groomer will draw on information they have gathered to target members of the victim's family.

They might, for example, say that failure to carry out a crime will end in their mum having an 'accident' at work or their brother being stabbed at school.

The effect is to both draw the target closer to the gang while isolating them from all other sources of potential support.

If they are afraid to turn to their family, teachers or authority figures, the groomer (and eventually the gang) will become the sole source of security. Naturally, this protection is never given freely.

Intervening in and Disrupting the Grooming Process

Just as in other gang awareness and prevention programmes, I believe that the earlier we can intervene and teach young people and their families how to avoid being groomed online and how to report concerns (e.g. locating and using the CEOP reporting service), the less likely it is that they will be duped into making poor decisions.

However, it is also crucial to identify those young people who are currently being groomed and to understand that the grooming process itself can make these young people evasive and hostile when it comes to co-operating with the authorities and wider community.

The process of grooming for sexual exploitation and grooming for gang recruitment are so similar that some of the findings from investigations of the former can be applied to the latter.

For example, a 2014 report from Overview & Scrutiny (Birmingham City Council) revealed that the time period over which grooming can occur varies widely.

In some cases, grooming can take months while in others only days are required (one case of grooming took just five days)

In addition, some of the warning signs of grooming activity are valid in both sexual exploitation and gang recruitment, including:

- ✓ Being contacted by strangers via social media
- ✓ Spending time alone with strangers
- ✓ Being invited to social gatherings which involve predominantly adults (like the parties I attended in north London)
- ✓ Receiving presents (phones, clothes, jewellery, etc.) from new 'friends.'

In all cases of grooming, the main objective is promoting trust for the purposes of carrying out criminal activities.

Therefore, interventions designed to tackle grooming in sex exploitation cases could – and maybe should – also focus on gang recruitment.

CHAPTER 5: The Gang Mentality

One of the biggest dilemmas in tackling gangs is over how gang members and gang-related crimes are referred to publicly, especially in the media and popular culture.

This is because of the 'badge of honour' mentality that is prevalent within gangs. Given this mentality, media coverage (in the case of news reports and documentaries), dramatic interpretations (movies, song lyrics, TV series) and even word of mouth in the community and schools can fan the fire of gang trouble.

Activities: Gangs in the Media

Discuss This!

- ✓ Which films can you name that include gangs?
- ✓ How are the gang members portrayed?
- ✓ Are they rich or poor? Healthy or sick? Respected or ridiculed?
- ✓ Why do you think the film-makers portrayed gangs in that way?
- ✓ How did the film end for the gang members?
- ✓ How do you think life ends for real gang members?

Try This!

Over a weekend, watch one film containing gangs and one documentary (these should be age appropriate. For example, some of the Harry Potter films feature the Death Eaters which could be seen as a gang).

1. How did you feel after watching the film? Did you want to be in a gang?
2. How about after watching the documentary?
3. What did the documentary include that the film left out?

For individuals who seek respect and a reputation (which I believe is the main driver of gang recruitment in current times), the creation of widespread fear and awe is positive reinforcement serving to make the gang life even more attractive and rewarding.

The gang identity thrives on this notion of respect with members craving this from their fellow gang members and achieving it through the intimidation of rivals and non-members.

So how do gang members actually win the respect they desire? This comes about through a willingness to carry out certain behaviours which serve to enhance their reputation.

Some of these behaviours may be ordered by the gang while others might be carried out autonomously with the intention of impressing the rest of the crew.

Some Examples of Gang Behaviour Carried Out to Earn Respect, Include:

- ✓ Derogatory comments or graffiti about rival gangs or gang members.
- ✓ Defacing a rival gang's graffiti.
- ✓ Displaying a weapon in the presence of a rival gang.
- ✓ Causing problems (or sometimes just showing up) in a rival gang's territory (including virtual turf such as a rival gang's website).
- ✓ Ripping off a rival gang in a drugs deal.
- ✓ Selling drugs on the rival's 'turf.'
- ✓ Hurting or intimidating a rival gang member's family.

Of course, these acts of disrespect then trigger a response. Even if the rival gang doesn't respond immediately, the animosity will continue to build until an act of revenge has been carried out.

This response could be as minor as petty vandalism or as major as a gun battle (in which innocent bystanders can be tragically affected).

This sparks a never-ending cycle of gang rival violence which inevitably escalates until serious injury or death to one or more gang members occurs. This is, of course, one of the main reasons why gangs are of such concern to police and the wider community.

In some areas, especially where gangs have become ingrained in the community, the line between a bona fide gang member and someone who has a friend or family connection to one or more gang members becomes blurred.

The gang influence can extend beyond the gang itself and become partially or fully embraced by non-members so that they may respond to threats, violence or disrespect in a similar way to how a gang member would.

This is where broad definitions of gangs can end up with numerous people from one community becoming tarred with the same brush.

The Structure of a Gang

Gangs often have a very clear and organised structure, and this is one of the criteria used for defining a gang in the UK.

In Angelique Flemming's book, 'Preventing Weapon Crime and Gang Membership,' she sets out the seven tiers of a typical gang – as researched by Urban Dynamics.

These are:

Gang leader. The gang leader is at the top of a hierarchical, authoritarian structure. They will make most of the day-to-day decisions and set the level of criminal activity depending largely on their personal characteristics.

Hardcore members. The most entrenched members of a gang, these members will generally be older, more violent and less likely to seek escape from the gang. They see the gang and associated crime as their life.

Associate members. These are committed gang members who use the hardcore members as their role models.

Clique members. These are fringe, wanna-be or could-be members who are closely attached to one or more hardcore gang members. However, they are not themselves as committed to or entrenched within the gang as associate or hardcore members.

Fringe members. These gang members tend to join and leave gangs of their own free will. They are less committed to a specific gang than associate and hardcore members.

Wanna-be members. These are often young people who aspire to become part of a gang. They will usually carry out illegal activities as instructed or just to try and impress other gang members. Wanna-be members are often being actively groomed by older gang members and/or gang-associated peers.

Could-be members. These are children and young teenagers most at risk of becoming part of a gang. They may have siblings within gangs or live in an area with a strong gang presence.

Direct and Structural Violence

Gang violence can be seen as a combination of direct and structural violence. It arises from the 'system' of a gang in the same way as other forms of violence (war, torture, police abuse) emerge from their respective systems. Therefore, it can also be regarded as a type of systemic violence.

The Difference Between Direct and Structural Violence

Direct violence is carried out with the sole purpose of abusing, violating or harming another person. Direct violence is usually treated as a crime.

Structural violence (or institutionalised violence) is a pervasive form of violence which is carried out and justified as part of an institution's norms. The Nazi concentration camps and military bombing campaigns are both examples of structural violence. There are also more subtle forms of violence whereby certain groups are denied equal rights.

Gangs Use Violence to Achieve Many Different Ends, Including:

- ✓ Gaining turf or defending existing turf.
- ✓ Getting revenge for actions carried out against the gang or their members (this can include minor slights to respect).
- ✓ Recruiting new members.
- ✓ Preventing members from leaving.
- ✓ Punishing members for breaking rules (enforcement).
- ✓ Removing unwanted members.
- ✓ Enhancing reputation for power.
- ✓ Earning respect.
- ✓ Displaying dominance.

Weapon Use in Gang Conflict

One worrying trend in the use of violence by gangs in the UK is an apparent increase in knife possession.

It can be difficult to draw meaningful statistics due to differences in crime reporting trends but, according to official ONS statistics, there was an alarming jump up in knife crime in the UK from 28,427 offences in 2015 to 32,448 in 2016.

In an April 2017 Daily Telegraph report, Professor David Wilson, a criminology professor at Birmingham City University, former prison governor and author, said: "Without a doubt, we are seeing a lot more young people using knives in the context of gangs and organised crime."

In the United States, there is the added danger of violence involving the use of firearms.

According to the Gun Violence Archive, a non-profit organisation compiling statistics about firearms offences in the United States, gun crime rose from 53,726 to 58,851 incidents between 2015 and 2016.

Many of these incidents will have involved gang-related disputes and the vast majority of gun-related homicides involve gangs.

The tendency of UK gangs to draw influence from US gangs and carry out copycat crimes should be a stark warning as to how gang violence is likely to develop if we don't act together to stop it.

For more on knife crime, see my book: **'Getting Real with Guns and Knives'**

The Perpetrator Mentality

The structure of the gang creates an alternative reality for their members. It is similar to the military in that loyalty to the group must go beyond any other ties. To enable them to carry out violent actions, a gang must induce a 'perpetrator mentality' in its members. What does this mentality look like on the outside and feel like on the inside?

- ✓ Any anxiety is internalised, and the perpetrator appears confident.
- ✓ The perpetrator uses their victim status as fuel for their anger. Their sense of injustice is motivation for their actions.
- ✓ Their negative experience with authority figures leads to a deep hatred.
- ✓ Fear, pain and power combine to become a toxic potion.
- ✓ Drugs and drink may be used to remove inhibitions.
- ✓ Perpetrators downplay the damage they cause until they feel unaccountable for their actions.
- ✓ Perpetrators refuse to fully reflect on their actions.

To more fully understand the reality in which gangs and their members operate, the next chapter focuses on the so-called **'Three R's of Gang Life.'** These are Reputation, Respect and Retaliation

CHAPTER 6: The Three R's of Gang Life

In terms of gang awareness, this is probably the most important chapter of the book. There are many factors contributing to the gang phenomenon but the craving for a reputation seems to be a particularly powerful force behind modern youth street gangs.

Reputation

As we saw earlier, a gang is partly defined by its structure. It is a hierarchical structure where reputation determines a members position within it. Therefore, to increase their status within the gang (and by extension their lives) a member will always be looking for ways to increase their reputation (or 'rep').

Individual reputation is earned through violent and anti-social behaviours. The more dramatic these acts are, the more the gang as a whole becomes feared by the community. This in turn increases the reputation of all members of the gang.

This inevitable leads to deliberate acts of ruthlessness in order to increase a gang's notoriety.

All gang members are expected to preserve the reputation of the gang at all costs and will either be directed or will take it upon themselves to carry out violence in order to combat a real or perceived threat.

Should a gang lose its reputation, it won't rest until it has re-established it. The same goes for an individual gang member who may have to prove him or herself to regain their position in the hierarchy.

Respect

Being treated with respect is a boost to self-esteem, one of the higher tiers in Maslow's Hierarchy of Needs theory.

Young people need to feel respected and the gang structure is in a position to provide this. To affirm their position, gang members will demand to be treated with respect. They will also expect the same respect (often in the form of fear) from non-gang members. Respect is also critically important for the gang as a whole since a lack of respect is a symptom of a loss of overall reputation.

The costs of maintaining respect are enormous. In the gang mentality, earning respect is synonymous with displaying courage, strength and ruthlessness – even going as far as to kill. Even where a gang is secure in their domination of an area, violence will be routinely used to reinforce their reputation and to keep order within the hierarchy.

Gang members might show disrespect for a rival gang in any number of ways. For example, they might spray over their graffiti with their own motifs, burn an item of clothing in the rival gang's colours or display a blade in front of a rival.

Retaliation

In gang culture, an attack to a gang's reputation is treated in the same way as a direct act of violence. Therefore, should a rival gang commit an act of disrespect, a refusal to respond would immediately be seen as weakness and would threaten the entire fabric that holds the gang together.

As such, there is no concept in gang life of letting an act of disrespect go unpunished. This is one of the most dangerous facets of the gang way of life because retaliation is inevitable, and the only question is how far the affronted gang or gang member will be prepared to go to get even.

In some cases, an act of vandalism against property may be considered adequate retaliation. In other situations, the gang may resort to arson or even to murder.

Retaliation is not restricted to rival gangs. If a gang feels disrespected or undermined by any group or individual they are likely to respond with violence.

For example, in some communities, citizens have been targeted for co-operating with the police in tackling gangs.

To summarise the above, every gang member is invested in building up a reputation for strength, bravado and ruthlessness. This will ensure they are held in high regard by other gang members who will demonstrate this by showing respect. Showing disrespect will inevitably lead to retaliation as the gang member looks to restore their reputation.

The same applies to the gang as a whole. A gang's reputation is tied up with its notoriety in the area and the reputation of its members. The gang demands to be treated with respect and any act of disrespect shown to a gang member by a rival gang (or other non-gang member) is perceived as an affront to the gang itself. The gang will then retaliate to reinforce their dominance.

Activities: Retaliation Tactics

Discuss This!

- ✓ What are the dangers of retaliation? Hint: How do you target the right person? When does it end?
- ✓ Is retaliation a show of strength or weakness? How about forgiveness?

Try This!

This is a variation of the famous Prisoner's Dilemma game.

1. Split into two groups: A and B
2. Each group has a card labelled Punish or Forgive.
3. After a count of three, each group must hold up a card with points allocated as follows:
4. If both cards are different, the team holding up Punish gets three points and the team holding up Forgive gets two points.
5. If both cards say Punish, nobody gets any points.
6. If both cards say Forgive, both teams get two points.
7. The winning team is the first to get to exactly ten points.

The rationale behind this game is that any team who wants to win will eventually have to play the Forgive card. (The game can be spiced up by presenting some age-appropriate scenarios).

Case Study: Being in the Wrong Place

Sometimes, gang retaliation claims the lives of innocent people simply because they happened to be in the wrong postcode area, wearing the wrong type of clothing at the wrong time.

According to various reports from the BBC, Evening Standard and Brent & Kilburn Times, Ice City Boyz rapper, Nines, allegedly the ringleader of a gang known as the Church Street Soldiers, performed online in a parody video in which he wore jewellery he claimed he had stolen from a north London rival, Cbiz.

In an apparent act of retaliation, a man wielding a Skorpion machine gun drove to the junction of Conley Street and Church Road where, shortly before 10pm on March 9th 2016, he shot dead 27-year-old Oliver Tetlow in what is believed to be a case of mistaken identity.

The feud doesn't seem to have ended there. An Ice City Boyz chain, allegedly stolen from rapper Keyz, was later displayed by 'gang members' on a YouTube video.

Cbiz and three co-defendants were later acquitted of Oliver's murder after a key witness changed their story and holes were found in the evidence.

No one has ever been found guilty and the machine gun, thought to have been smuggled down from Manchester, has never been recovered.

A Word of Warning

When working with gang members (or those at risk of becoming involved with gangs), naivety can be dangerous. Violence is so much a part of gang culture that there is a real danger that well-meaning individuals could get hurt or even killed.

When working with gangs, members of the community should be aware of the importance of respect and reputation in the gang's structure.

Failing to honour a gang member by showing them respect is likely to be met by aggressive posturing or outright violence.

Being openly critical or condescending about a gang member's actions or feelings, particularly in front of his or her 'crew' will not be taken lightly and could even insult the gang as a whole.

As I will go on to explain later in the book, showing that you respect a gang member's opinions and views, despite not sharing them, is a better way to maintain a relationship with a gang member or a young person on the fringe of a gang. It may even prevent them from being seduced by gang recruiters.

However, it is unwise to adopt the gang's posturing and clothing yourself in an attempt to build a connection. This in itself could be construed as a lack of respect (although is more likely to be mocked).

Being respectful while also being yourself is a much more effective way to earn mutual respect. That includes sticking to agreed meeting times and places (regardless of whether the gang member returns the courtesy).

Nevertheless, it is always wise to be on your guard when around gangs and to remove yourself from the situation if you sense any danger.

There is another important consideration that people working with young gang members must make. A successful attempt to extricate a gang member from the gang is likely to be seen as an act of disrespect by both the rescuing organisation and the gang member themselves.

The gang will be bound by their own code to retaliate and this could end with violence including injury or even death to the escapee gang member. In such cases, the legal position of the rescuing party may not bc clear cut, particularly if they are not trained in working with youth gangs.

CHAPTER 7: Common Traits of Gang Members

So, what does a typical gang member look like? What picture comes to mind when you think about a gang member?

As with any group, our perceptions are influenced by our experiences which might only include representations of gangs in the mass media (and these are often glamorised, particularly in the movies!)

In truth, appearances can be deceptive and, as we mentioned in the chapter on definitions, young people who look, act and dress similarly can be incorrectly labelled as gang members. It is also possible to miss the signs of gang influence because the child being groomed doesn't wear a bandana or talk about his 'bredren.'

What is more useful is to pull out some characteristics that the majority of gang members share. That is what this section is all about:

Gang Members are Often Looking for a Surrogate Family

When young people feel ignored, disrespected and vulnerable within their family and neighbourhood, the gang appears to offer an antidote. I have found that this desire to find a surrogate family is often strong with female gang members.

As detailed in the grooming section, prospective gang members are often offered protection from other gangs in return for their affiliation. They are also given plenty of attention and a road to becoming respected.

Gang Members Are Often from Broken Families

The breakdown of the traditional family unit has left many children without positive adult role models. Some of these children witness and experience domestic violence, drug abuse and sexual exploitation from a very young age. For these young people, gang life is hardly a culture shock. It's just a different version of what is normal for them.

A Craving for Identity and Recognition

Some young people go through life being told they are stupid, weak and lacking in talent. They slip through the net in school and achieve poor grades, suffer from bullying and miss out on the sports teams.

Where young people are struggling with feelings of low self-worth and failing in their attempts to achieve at school or, later, to get a job, the gang offers a means to gain a status to be somebody. Who wouldn't be attracted to that?

Within the gang, these young people can finally excel at something while giving vent to the anger and pain within.

Gang Members May Be in Need of Money

The benefits that come from gang affiliation are not just psychological in nature. There is real potential to make a short-term material profit – sometimes a very good one – from participating in gang activities.

Of course, these activities are criminal in nature and the financial compensation comes from sharing in the ill-gotten gains. Gang members share profits from drug trafficking, robberies, theft rings, illegal arms sales and other illegal activities.

Material wealth goes hand-in-hand with reputation within the gang structure. As new gang members rise up the ranks, established members get to enjoy more of the wealth and palm off much of the menial and risky criminal work to new recruits. These individuals become role models while younger members strive to achieve a higher position in the organisation through proving their worth.

Competing with the monetary allure that gangs have is a huge challenge for those wanting to tackle gangs in society. Gang members, especially those from deprived families in affluent neighbourhoods, may have grown up without the technology, fashionable clothing and other material trappings of their peers.

Why would gang members willingly return to a system which, in their eyes, brings them nothing but shame, vulnerability and poverty?

Gang Members Often Have History

Although not all gang members come from a family of criminals, many do. They may be carrying on a family tradition established by grandparents, uncles, aunts, cousins, parents and siblings whom they see as role models.

Gang Members Often Come from Deprived Neighbourhoods

Although gang members are also recruited from wealthy areas, we must face the fact that gang violence is more prevalent in the inner cities affected with poverty. We cannot also ignore the number of black youths whose lives have been cut short though various acts of violence (although it is a mistake to assume most gang members are black; there are also plenty of white and Asian gangs).

Poor areas are associated with more dysfunctional families, higher rates of unemployment, a greater likelihood of criminal role models and material deprivation. The gang life shines all the brighter in these areas with their offer of a surrogate family and a rapid means to earn a living and achieve material gains.

Gang Members Often Come from Violent Neighbourhoods Where Gangs are Established

In many cases, particularly where gangs are deeply rooted in an area, new recruits are pressurised into joining through violence or scare tactics.

Gangs may literally threaten to harm or kill a young person or their family if they don't join the gang. Alternatively, they might claim that a rival gang is planning to target them and the only way they can stay safe is by joining the gang for protection.

Gang Members Often Have Nowhere Else to Turn

In some cases, the decision to join a gang seems to be the only one – because it is a matter of life or death.

For example, where young people, through serious physical and sexual abuse, decide to run away from home, they are at the mercy of other people.

A gang can offer real safety in these cases, providing a roof, food to eat, clothing and protection from violence. Of course, this safe haven is not provided for free and young runaways are forced to engage in survival sex or criminal behaviour to stay safe.

Once these young, vulnerable people have become involved in crime, their range of choices narrow further since turning to the authorities could end up with them being jailed.

This is why decriminalisation of 'prostitution' and schemes whereby minor offences are overlooked can be effective in tackling the scourge of gangs.

Activities: Why Young People Join Gangs

Discuss This!

- ✓ Do you think young people always have a choice whether to join a gang or not?
- ✓ What do you think are the main reasons young people join gangs?
- ✓ Do you think certain ethnic groups are portrayed more as gang members than others? Explain your answer.

CHAPTER 8: Gang Fashion & Behaviour

Displaying their sense of unique identity is central to every gang. Clothing, posture, hairstyle and body art are some of the conspicuous ways in which gang members identify one another and distance themselves from rival gangs.

Gang Dress Code

Similar to other kinds of group, a gang's dress code can range from highly individual and flexible to strict and formal. In either case, adopting the gang's dress code is regarded as a display of loyalty.

As detailed in an earlier chapter, the concept of respect is central to the reputation of a gang. One of the ways in which a rival gang will show disrespect is by parodying the dress code (making a joke out of it) or by burning or otherwise vandalising items of clothing in their rivals' colours. This will, of course, provoke a swift retaliation.

A gang's dress code can cause problems for innocent members of the community. For example, if a person were to inadvertently wear clothes or colours of a similar style to a local gang, they might be mistaken for a gang member and targeted by rivals of that gang.

In addition, some police officers might judge young people to be part of a gang simply because they are wearing a particular style of clothing that they recognise as being similar to that worn by specific gangs. If those youths are also engaged in criminal behaviour, they could find themselves on the end of a gang-related charge with a much heftier sentence.

Gang Hairstyles and Tattoos

Just like the military, some gangs will have rules regarding the kind of hairstyle their members should wear. They may also order members to have a tattoo incorporating their gang's unique insignia and/or colours.

Of course, tattoos are becoming a popular sight on UK streets with many young men and women sporting them. However, tattoos have always been one of the ways in which gang members have displayed their allegiance.

Gangs will vary in how prescriptive their rules are when it comes to clothing, hair and body art with traditional street gangs tending to be stricter than looser structures (e.g. hybrid gangs).

Gang Clothing

As with youth culture itself, fashion trends change over time and certain items of clothing may be more prominent in some countries and cities than others.

The following list should be seen as a general guide:

Beanie hats and baseball caps. These may be in the colour of the affiliated gang and may be embroidered with symbols/signs. Gang members might wear their hats tilted to one side or backwards. These are not always arbitrary decisions.

Gangs may associate themselves with a left or right orientation and members would then tilt their cap to the appropriate direction.

Bandanas. These are a common item of gang fashion as they can be used to make a statement and hide the face.

Masks/Balaclavas. Another way to hide the face and create fear.

Designer Clothing. Older gang members, particularly those from west London, like to flaunt their wealth. They are often seen wearing Moncler puffer jackets and clothes by Gucci, Louis Vuitton, Fendi and Christian Louboutin.

Tracksuits & Puffer Jackets. Younger gang members, especially those from south London and other deprived areas can often be seen wearing tracksuits and puffer jackets.

Expensive trainers. Younger gang members may show off their expensive Nike trainers as a mark of wealth.

Hoodies. There is a practical use for the hoodie: it can be pulled up to hide a gang member's features.

Jewellery. Gang-related jewellery is both an overt show of material wealth and another way in which a gang can display its symbols, colours and/or initials.

All of the above fashion items apply equally to males and females in gangs.

It is important to understand that many of the clothes mentioned above are worn by non-gang members too. For example, rich young people, dancers and footballers also wear expensive designer clothing and backwards-facing caps, etc.

Case Study: The Borough Wars of South London

This case study illustrates the central importance of gang colours and postcode in an area of London with an established gang culture.

In 2009, according to the Evening Standard, a battle involving more than 60 youths broke out in the borough of Lewisham, known as the 'blue borough' due to the colour of its logo, signs, bins and lampposts. The fight involved gangs from Lewisham and Penge. There are signs on the border of Penge which say, 'Welcome to the Green Borough.'

Teenager Ben Hitchcock was with members of the Penge gang as they arrived at a birthday party near Beckenham High Street. After initial hostilities, a large group of 'blues,' armed with bats, bottles and knives engaged the 'greens.' In the aftermath, Ben lost his life after being stabbed in the back. Ben had been attired in white, a fact which was described as 'noticeably rude' by the young teenage girl who had thrown the party.

Some of the gangs from Lewisham include Brockley Mandem, Deptford Boys, Deptford Marlies, Ghetto Boys, Monson Bloodset, The Money Makers and Young Money Makers.

The Ghetto Boys have a long-term rivalry with the Peckham Boys.

Peckham, in the south-east London district of Southwark, is often known as the 'black borough.' Its members wear black clothing including bandanas which may be worn around the lower face, neck or wrist. Young members from a Peckham gang were behind the 'manslaughter' of ten-year old schoolboy Damilola Taylor which became one of the most high-profile gang-related killings in the country.

Gang Body Art

Gang members often display their signs, colours, gang name and/or mottos via tattoos. Wearing an obvious gang tattoo is a clear show of commitment and, unlike more ambiguous clothing, is usually a clear sign that the wearer is a 'signed and paid up' gang member.

One way in which schools can reduce the influence of gangs – at least within their gates – is to enforce a strict dress code which doesn't allow extreme hair or clothing styles and restricts the wearing of jewellery. However, this will only address one relatively minor symptom of the wider gang problem.

Criminal and Antisocial Behaviour

Gang leaders will also control the behaviours of rank-and-file members to a greater or lesser extent.

Criminal behaviours inevitably form part of a gang's repertoire of activities. Although gangs are associated with serious criminal acts such as arson, robbery, assault and murder, they may also indulge in relatively minor offences such as vandalism, petty theft and displaying intimidating behaviour.

This is particularly the case with younger gang members where such acts of antisocial behaviour may form part of gang initiation prior to more serious crimes.

Drawing the line between what is general juvenile delinquency and what is gang-related antisocial behaviour can be difficult.

Graffiti and Gang Signs

One specific type of anti-social behaviour which is strongly associated with gangs is graffiti because this is one way in which gangs assert their presence in an area and challenge rival gangs over territory. However, it can be difficult to tell real gangster-related graffiti apart from general delinquent behaviour, tagging, or even genuine street art.

Influence of Music

Certain styles of urban music are often associated with gangs and there are particular sub-genres of hip hop which can help to propagate gang culture. These include grime from the UK and trap and drill music, originally from the USA but now popular in the UK.

Grime emerged from inner city London, from the jungle and garage dance scenes, and is also influenced by ragga and hip hop. Tracks typically feature fast, syncopated breakbeats and gritty urban lyrics. Grime is sometimes described as aggressive and raw. Some of its most well-known musicians are Dizzee Rascal,

Skepta and Stormzy. The reputation of grime clubs for attracting trouble has allegedly led to them being specifically targeted by the police.

Trap music is named after the 'traps' where drug deals are done. The style is characterised by layered synthesisers, a fast beat, a brooding atmosphere and lyrics revolving around poverty, drugs and life in the 'trap.' Drill music, a variation of Trap is particularly raw and violent and aggressive in its delivery.

Activities: Music and Gangs

Discuss This!

- ✓ Why do you think music is such an important part of gang culture?
- ✓ What are the dangers of associating a type of music with gangs?
- ✓ Can music make the gang problem worse? Why?
- ✓ Can music help save communities from gangs? How?

Try This!

In response to the trouble associated with some clubs featuring DJs and MCs, the police created a form (form 696). Print out some copies of this form.

1. Divide the class into two groups. One group will play the supporters and one the critics of Form 696.
2. Give each group ten minutes to come up with arguments supporting and criticising the use of Form 696.
3. Both groups should present their argument in a class debate.

4. For an additional activity, the class could design an improved form.

Try This!

Create a piece of music in the grime or trap style but with a positive message. Be careful about the lyrics and imagery if presenting examples to young people. These need to be age appropriate.

Dealing with Gang-Type Behaviour in Children

The glamorisation of gangs in the mass media together with young people's healthy need to explore their identities and push boundaries has led gangsters to become a fashionable style icon.

Many young people will start listening to grime music, wear gangster-style clothing and speak in gangster lingo. In thc vast majority of cases this is completely harmless. Just because a young person is listening to grime and acting like a 'gangsta' it doesn't follow that they are in any risk of becoming part of a gang.

However, when children are emulating gang fashion and behaviour it is a good opportunity to question them about their views on gangs and why they are attracted to the scene.

This can provide a useful window into the psychological attraction that the gangster persona holds for young people. It is best not to be confrontational as this will likely drive them away or cause them to shut down.

Likewise, when it comes to tattoos, the decision to have one is, on its own, no indication of gang involvement. However, it may be worth asking why a son, daughter or student has opted for a particular design. If they are evasive or they reveal that the tattoo is related to a local gang, this is a cause for concern.

Of course, where a child is engaging in antisocial behaviour, this should always be treated as a serious matter. Even if they are not yet involved in gangs, disruptive behaviour is a sign that something is not right in that person's world.

Significantly, it also indicates a weakening of the ties which bond young people to their community. Just like a lamb straying from the herd, a delinquent youth is vulnerable to being targeted by the predatory 'wolves' of a gang on the hunt for new blood.

Looking at What Is Missing

When young people swagger around like a gangster or throw a rock through a window, what are they really saying?

Children who are confident in themselves don't feel the need to adopt the customs, attitudes or clothing of another. Young people who are materially and emotionally fulfilled gain no pleasure from destroying the property of others.

Rather than obsess over the negative behaviours which our youths are engaging in, might it be more beneficial to look at what is missing from their lives and how we, as a society, can provide them with what they need?

For example, are we doing enough to provide a variety of activities and opportunities for young people from difficult backgrounds or do we exclude them (financially or emotionally)? Are we supporting them to overcome their problems or turning away and ignoring them? Are we tackling discrimination and prejudice against people from certain cultural and/or economic backgrounds?

After all, it is a sad reflection of society if gangs become the only groups in which a young person can find a sense of belonging.

CHAPTER 9: Mental Health & Gang Pressures

Growing up in London, I was very paranoid and fearful of my life as a teenager. Falling victim to gang knife or gun crime was always on the back of my mind. Would I be the next person to fall fate?

I believe most of my peers shared the same view but because of the male ego we never spoke about the mental struggles we faced. It was something you basically had to deal with: the concept of survival of the fittest.

Everybody I knew, from secondary school to college, had some form of a weapon. This was not necessarily to be the aggressor. In fact, 90 per cent of the time it was more as a form of protection.

The common saying then was: "It's better to be judged by 12 than carried by 6". The findings of the Impact Report from the Ben Kinsella Trust back up my own experiences. One in seven of the young people attending the Trust's exhibitions revealed that they know someone who carries a knife.

It should come as no surprise then that mental health issues are strongly entwined with the gang phenomenon. Personality disorders, depression and obsessive-compulsive disorder (OCD) are just some of the common mental health illnesses suffered by those vulnerable young people in gangs or at risk of joining one.

In addition, some of the criminal activities that a young gang member may witness or be involved in perpetrating can leave a mental scar. For example, being forced to watch a gang murder or to stab or shoot someone can lead to post-traumatic stress disorder (PTSD).

I myself watched friends change as they wilfully chose to be involved in gangs. Even though, from the outside, they looked cool, wore expensive jewellery and clothes and drove flashy sports cars. I also saw the mental health side of things behind closed doors. There was paranoia and increased substance abuse to help ease the pressures of gang involvement.

The UK government's 'Dying to Belong,' report recognised the importance of tackling what they called the 'drivers' of gang culture, listing mental and emotional health problems among them. They recommended early intervention, partly through providing greater access to bespoke mental health services for children and adolescents. I too believe early intervention is critical in beating the gangs.

Mental health professionals play an important role in gang interventions partly because their goals are focused on helping the individual to achieve psychological and emotional health. This can be a welcome breath of fresh air for a gang member used to feeling ignored or actively ground down by parents and peers while being treated as a source of trouble by the authorities.

Mentally and emotionally healthy youths do not tend to join gangs so, despite a lack of scientific study, positive mental health interventions should not be underestimated in their ability to tackle gangs and create positive change in the community.

Although admitting the evidence is mainly anecdotal in nature, Saul Levine and George Montoya in their book, 'Juveniles in Gangs,' vouch for the efficacy of a wide range of different psychotherapeutic interventions such as psychodynamic therapies, interactional therapy, pharmacotherapy, client-centred therapy, CBT (already discussed in a previous chapter) and family therapy.

So Which Approach is Better?

According to Levine and Montoya, each approach has its strengths and weaknesses and ultimate success is less to do with the therapeutic model and more to do with the 'chemistry' between service providers and gang members; ancillary interventions and individual characteristics of the gang member themselves. Although this paints a rather ad-hoc picture it does at least provide hope that we can rescue some of our young people.

Perhaps future research on the specifics of this service provider/gang member chemistry might ensure a more thoughtful approach to pairing therapists with their patients.

Referring Pupils to Mental Health Services

The US Department of Justice Report, 'Changing Course: Preventing Gang Membership,' report recommended that mental health professionals should be placed in schools as a priority in order to identify the need for psychological help and to deliver or co-ordinate those services.

As well as identifying existing youth gang members and 'at risk' children, it may be necessary to deliver support to the wider school community in areas where the influence of gangs is very notable. This situation can cause chronic stress throughout the school and community as a whole.

It should be pointed out that students must be appropriately treated and while pastoral care, counselling and various therapies all have their benefits, they may not be suitable where children are displaying symptoms of serious psychological issues.

Specific mental illnesses such as PTSD will require more specialist interventions than most schools can provide. Trying to treat these illnesses without the appropriate academic training in place can lead to further suffering and damage.

For UK teachers concerned that their own counselling services are inadequate to deal with problematic behaviour in children, a referral can be made to Child and Adolescent Mental Health Services (CAMHS).

CAMHS is an NHS service which includes a variety of health professionals, for example:

- ✓ counsellors;
- ✓ family therapists;
- ✓ occupational therapists;
- ✓ outreach workers.
- ✓ primary mental health workers;
- ✓ psychologists;

- ✓ psychotherapists;
- ✓ social workers;

Be aware that there can be a long waiting list for this service so be sure to follow up and formally complain if necessary. You can complain to NHS England or the area's clinical commissioning group (CCG) if you are still not satisfied.

Mental Health Issues Within the Family

Where strong family risk factors are apparent (high truancy rates, lack of parental involvement, neglect, etc.) mental health interventions aimed at the family level (e.g. family therapy) may be beneficial.

For example, in some deprived areas, there are many single parents. Being a single parent is tough and can lead to high levels of stress, social isolation and accompanying mental illness.

The burden of debt and of trying to juggle work and family can be overwhelming with problems magnified when there is only one adult dealing with them.

Although it would be wrong to tar all single parents with one brush, single parents living with their own mental health problems are likely to be less nurturing to their children and more likely to treat them harshly. This can contribute to feelings of low self-worth and internalised anger in the child.

Where the risk of maltreatment is high, evidence presented in the Changing Course report tends to show that the most successful form of intervention are those which start early, involve home visitation and treat family health and wellbeing as a whole.

Programmes delivered by professional visitors (e.g. nurses and mental health workers) were found to be more effective than those delivered by paraprofessionals although long-term paraprofessional support (two years or more) also benefited children in such families.

Rather than treating individual mental health problems in isolation, such programmes covered physical health, nutrition, employment, education and social connections.

This is a common theme running through gang interventions: multi-faceted, multi-agency approaches seem to be far more effective in tackling gangs than single solution methods.

Employment and Mental Health

The 'Dying to Belong' report also highlighted the research connecting work with positive mental health.

When people are in fulfilling employment they develop improved self-esteem, build social connections and are able to work towards the future they desire.

Part of tackling gang culture has to focus on improving employment prospects for young people in deprived areas. The quality of jobs as well as the quantity has to be addressed.

CHAPTER 10: Female Sexual Exploitation

Girls in Gangs: Correcting A Myth

Traditionally, females are reported to make up less than 10 per cent of the entire gang population. The few sources available suggest that female participation is significantly under-reported.

The Changing Course report claims that the involvement of girls in gangs is hugely underestimated and that the ratio of girls to boys in gangs is now between a quarter and a third; I would estimate a quarter from my experiences. The findings of the Denver Youth Survey, a longitudinal study of urban youth, puts the figure at between one-sixth and a half.

Sexual Exploitation of Females by Male Gang Members

Research also suggests that females in gangs are more likely to experience sexual abuse and exploitation than males and that, regardless of whether they are bona fide members, girls associated with gangs are nevertheless at high risk.

A study from Texas, quoted in a 2003 report: 'Risk Behaviours among Young Mexican-American Gang-Associated Females: sexual relations, partying, substance use, and crime,' concluded, "regardless of their relationship to the gang, all the females were prone to some degree of substance use, crime and high-risk sexual behaviour."

The Changing Course report highlights how girls in gangs tend to identify more with male gang members than with other females in the gang hierarchy. This leads them to enable and, in some cases, actively take part in the sexual exploitation of other girls. For example, girl gang members might:

- ✓ Ignore male gang member violence towards female gang members and girlfriends.
- ✓ Blame female members for male infidelity.
- ✓ Use their sexual appeal to set up rival gang members (a honey-trap).
- ✓ Set up other girls for sexual assault.

Of course, the above research is specific to the United States, but it would be a mistake to think that girls are not equally involved in gangs in the UK.

Media reports in the UK mirror many of these findings with girl gang members even admitting to setting up friends for sexual abuse in order to obtain money from the gang.

I have personally found that female gang members often show pride at being in a relationship with the most respected gang members and will often fight to preserve that status.

Rescuing Girls from Sexual Exploitation in Gangs

Despite their experience of abuse by male gang members, it is often perceived to be a fair price to pay for the security and acceptance the gang structure provides. In interviews with female gang members, many report that they joined a gang because they were looking for a surrogate family following early childhood experiences of sexual abuse, parental neglect, alcoholism, substance misuse and other issues.

It is therefore unsurprising that girls undervalue the extent of their abuse within gangs – to them it is part of normality. They may also hold on to the conviction that their abusers are genuine boyfriends.

Here are some statistics gathered from various US studies into female gang members and sexual abuse:

- ✓ Proportion of gang members who have experienced (mainly familial) sexual assault: 52-62%
- ✓ Proportion of non-gang members who have experienced (mainly familial) sexual assault: 22%
- ✓ Proportion of sexual abuse victims who are female: 71%

Where family abuse is intolerable, girls may end up on the streets. Such female child runaways form a vulnerable group making up a large proportion of gang members. One, albeit very dated, report from Los Angeles found that three-quarters of female gang members had run away from home.

This was more than double the proportion of male gang members. Runaways may be forced into survival sex or groomed into gangs by the offer of physical and emotional support.

These complications, together with other factors such as the characteristics of neighbourhood in which the girls are growing up, mean that attempts to extricate exploited girls from gangs must be handled with the same sensitivity and multi-agency approach as any other gang intervention.

However, due to the differences in the pattern of risk factors between male and female gang members, gender-specific interventions may be necessary.

Some organisations have formed gender-specific teams focusing on reaching female gang members through strengths-based strategies or cognitive-behavioural therapy (CBT). For example, the Changing Course report features the work of Maryland's Female Intervention Team (FIT).

Some strategies the FIT use include having guest speakers from the gang members' community. These women tell inspiring stories of how they have overcome sexual exploitation and other difficult life circumstances in the hope that female gang members will follow in their footsteps.

It is also clear that interventions need to be aimed at tackling sexual abuse and neglect within the family. The sooner 'at risk' children are identified and, where necessary, removed from their toxic family environments, the less likely it will be that they will seek out the company of gangs.

One of the interventions aimed at very young children is Canada's SNAP Girls (Stop Now and Plan) programme which has been running, in its current form, since the mid-Nineties. SNAP Girls works with children between the ages of 6 and 11 who have begun to display problematic behaviour. It uses a feminist approach to gender difference and aims to use CBT to instil self-control so that girls can think before they act.

Another example is the Safe Dates programme. This is an American middle and high school-based intervention aimed at raising awareness of what healthy and abusive dating looks like. To close this section, I want to emphasise that my highlighting the increased risk of sexual exploitation of girls in gangs isn't intended to reduce girls' participation in gangs to that of sex objects.

Girls can be every bit as independent and autonomous as male gang members and will face the same pressure to maintain their reputation within the organisation through using violence and committing serious crime.

In fact, a study by Ebensen and colleagues revealed that gangs with female members tended to be more organised than those without. It is also important not to assume that girls from different cultural backgrounds come into gangs with the same set of attitudes and experiences. For example, studies have shown that African American women in gangs are less likely to see men in a positive light than Latino women.

However, there is little doubt that females bear the brunt of sexual exploitation and that gangs enable and perpetrate abuse through grooming and sexually motivated initiation rituals.

CHAPTER 11: Drugs, Child Trafficking and County Lines

We cannot deny that gang violence has a direct correlation to drugs and substance abuse. Gangs and the illegal drugs trade are closely intertwined. Drugs form both a means of income and a way by which members can become dependent on the gang.

Drug use is also seen as normal by many young people who end up joining gangs because many of them have parents who have used and/or dealt in illegal substances. In a sense they are born into the drugs trade.

Gangs and The Drugs Trade

Drugs are a lucrative source of income for many street gangs. As a result, a lot of importance is placed on securing control over the supply of drugs in specific areas – right down to street level.

With drugs comes violence. 'Turf wars' are often fought on these boundaries as gangs look to reclaim, consolidate or expand their territories.

Therefore, the all-important reputation of a gang depends heavily on their perceived presence in an area. The more widespread and established a gang is, the more drugs they will be in control of and the more money they will be earning.

To disrupt the activities and attack the reputation of a gang, a rival might set up a 'rip off' deal where drugs are stolen or fake drugs supplied. This will attract the inevitable retaliation which too often ends in serious injury or death.

It should be pointed out that not all gangs deal in drugs. The code of some gangs forbids the trafficking of narcotics.

However, most gangs take advantage of this means to make money quickly and may actively establish links with major international drug trafficking organisations or even compete with them.

Business and Drug Gangs

Some gangs specialise in the profiteering side, their wider gang culture used mainly as a cover for their criminal businesses. While some business gangs diversify their trade by dealing in arms, prostitution and slaves others carve out a niche in the drugs trade.

Drug gangs tend to be comprised mainly of older gang members and are extremely violent, fiercely competitive over territory and market share. People working with youths in drug gangs may be particularly at risk.

Young People as Drugs Runners and Lookouts

Young boys and girls are the ideal choice when it comes to carrying drugs between buyers and sellers or to and from safe houses for the following reasons:

- ✓ **Less risk of being searched.** A disrupted drug deal is a major inconvenience to a gang. As well as the obvious financial hit, they end up with unhappy customers and, worst of all, a smeared reputation. Gang members know that children and young teens are less likely to be stopped and their bags or clothes searched by the police. That's why they routinely get young people to do their dirty work.
- ✓ **Less risk of arrest**. A young gang member is an asset to the gang and they want to keep them on the streets as much as possible. Even if a young drug runner is arrested they are more likely to get away with a ticking off. This makes them available for the next deal.
- ✓ **More expendable**. If a young gang member is taken to a prison, injured or killed, older members higher up the hierarchy are protected.
- ✓ **Less knowledgeable**. Young gang members are less likely to be able to provide useful information to the authorities when arrested.
- ✓ **Gateway to serious crimes**. A young gang member can prove their worth to the gang by being a reliable drug runner. When they are more established members they will be phased into carrying out more serious and usually violent crimes.
- ✓ **Easily manipulated.** It is far easier for an older gang member to threaten, bribe or flatter a vulnerable child or young teen to do their bidding than someone of their own age.
- ✓ **Gateway to drug use**. If a young gang member can become addicted to drugs they become both more dependent on the gang and a source of income. It is in a gang's interest to encourage drug addiction. Young girls can be more easily pressurised into sexual activity if they are addicted to drugs. This can also be a source of income to gangs who deal in prostitution.

- ✓ **Easier to use as lookouts**. Other young gang members may act as lookouts during a drug deal, warning the gang when they spot signs of the police.

Activities: The Role of Youngers

Discuss This!

Being asked to carry drugs for a big gang boss is exciting and can make young people feel special.

- ✓ Imagine you are a gang boss. Why would you choose a younger to carry drugs? Is it because you think they're special or because you don't care if they go to jail as long as you get the money.
- ✓ Do they protect you from the danger of being attacked by rivals?

County Lines and Child Trafficking

In addition to running their local drugs trade, many city drug dealers, for example those based in London, Liverpool and Birmingham, operate several 'county lines.' These are extended drug dealing networks focusing on small towns, rural and coastal areas.

The term is thought to arise from both the single line of communication from a dealers 'burner' phone to their city contact and the notion of 'crossing county lines' to escape law enforcement, a phrase borrowed from America.

County lines are a growing concern to police forces throughout the country both due to the effect on local communities and the large number of teens and young children being used to carry the drugs.

County lines is often a form of child trafficking with children as young as 11 (but normally young teenagers) groomed through bribery with money, clothes and sex.

These youths are then separated from their families and taught the tools and techniques needed for surviving 'OT' (out there) including how to use a 'burner' phone to avoid being tracked, how to carry drugs inside their bodies through swallowing or 'plugging' them, how to market drugs to the target community and how to 'cuckoo.' This is the practice of latching on to local drug users (nitties) or other vulnerable people (e.g. adults with learning difficulties) for use of their property as a base.

Once established in an area, county lines may diversify to encompass prostitution and other illicit trades.

The War Against Drugs

Most people agree that drugs are a menace to society and lead to violence and broken communities. However, there is less agreement over how to deal with them.

Some people and groups take the zero tolerance and strict enforcement approach. The anti-drug policies of Rodrigo Duterte, the president of the Philippines is an extreme example of this position.

Others take the polar opposite view, believing that decriminalising or even legalising drugs is the only way to remove the financial power the gangs are wielding.

Then there is the educational approach. This focuses on working with families and individual young people – in their homes and at schools – to build up their self-esteem and awareness to a point where they won't be tempted into using drugs.

Educational programmes may be run by schools, local authorities, the police, public health bodies or private companies.

Parents can help by staying informed about drug use in their area and remaining alert to the presence of drugs and associated paraphernalia in their environment (e.g. suspicious items in their children's rooms or drug-related discussions in social media or chat applications).

Not all youth drug taking involves overt gang membership, but it does support the drugs industry which, in turn, ruins lives.

Case Study: The Deadly Link Between Gangs and Drugs

In a previous case study, I detailed the tragic death of Oliver Tetlow in Brent, north London.

In November 2017, over a year and a half after the shooting, one of the men acquitted for Oliver's murder was arrested in Llandudno, North Wales.

According to news reports, he was found in possession of a large quantity of heroin and crack cocaine. He was reported as claiming he was selling the drugs to pay off a student debt.

This case serves to highlight the links between gangs and drugs and also to show how gangs are not just an inner-city problem.

CHAPTER 12: Spotting General Risk Factors

Unfortunately, for those looking to tackle gang-associated problems, at-risk youths don't come with neon signs saying, 'deprived background,' 'dysfunctional family,' or 'threatened with violence.'

However, there are several indicators which can help us to notice when individuals may be at risk of joining a gang.

Family Indicators

There may be signs that a particular individual is experiencing difficulties at home. Of course, this doesn't necessarily mean they are being abused and are going to run away and join a gang. However, the following should be seen as potential red flags, particularly if two or more are present:

Stressful Family Life

Sometimes family stress is clear to see the moment you step into someone's home. At other times the signs are more subtle. For example, a child may seem unnaturally fearful of their parents or angry with their siblings.

If you are a teacher, you might notice that a young child does not show the usual excitement at 'picking up time.'

Parental Non-Involvement and Low Expectations

Parents may be conspicuously absent in some homes with young people given free rein to live their lives how they want. Some people in gang-afflicted communities describe how children are allowed to 'raise themselves.'

Without the strong voice of the family, how can young, impressionable people ignore the voices of the gang elders who convince them to carry knives for self-defence or make a living through selling drugs?

Indicators are parents who regularly fail to attend Parents' Evenings and other important school events. When they are present, they may be overly critical of their child and compare them negatively with other children.

Low Parental Education Level

Parents of vulnerable children may themselves be vulnerable and come across as having borderline learning difficulties.

Abuse and Neglect

This can be difficult to spot. Victims and perpetrators become skilled at hiding the physical evidence while emotional harm shows no outward scars. Unexplained injuries, regular absences and a general lack of care (ill-fitting clothes, scruffy hair, low body weight, begrimed appearance) may signify abuse and/or neglect.

Ineffective Parenting

Some young people exhibit behavioural problems from a very early age with their parents seemingly powerless to control them. This is a cause for real concern. There could be physical or sexual abuse occurring behind the scenes and the parents may be enabling this through being inattentive or too concerned about their own lives. Programs such as SNAP in Canada aim to work with children as young as six who may be already at risk of joining gangs.

Parents with a Criminal Background

Parents who are regularly in trouble with the authorities may be involved in gang activities themselves.

Personal Indicators

Even where there is limited knowledge about an individual's family background, their overall attitude and behaviour can indicate a vulnerability to gang affiliation.

Low Motivation and No Aspirations

If young people are disengaged with their education and community activities their school work will suffer and they will become side-lined in society. These individuals may see the gang way of life as the only option for getting on in life.

Low Self-Esteem

Young people with low self-esteem are vulnerable to being groomed into gang affiliation. Groomers will simultaneously reinforce a person's worthlessness while providing the means – through violence and criminality – to earn respect.

Behavioural/Discipline Problems

Acting up at school can signify a dysfunctional family background – a big risk factor for future gang membership. Serious forms of criminal behaviour and violence could indicate that a child is already carrying out gang orders or proving themselves ahead of initiation.

Alcohol or Drug Use

Substance abuse can be used to mask problems at home and can also indicate that a young person is being supplied with alcohol and/or drugs by gangs.

Poor Peer Relations

Young people with no one else to turn to may find a willing ear in a local gang member. Lack of self-reflection/self-awareness. If a young person is unable to learn lessons from their experiences they are at risk of making bad life choices.

Community Indicators

Family and personal risk factors can be overcome when communities come together to provide the facilities and support services young people need to succeed and feel good about themselves. However, where these safety nets are missing there is a potential for gangs to fill those gaps.

Lack of Community Support Services

Individuals and schools need to have somewhere to turn to for support. Where such service provision is poor, children have nowhere to go and schools feel unsupported.

High Crime Rate

Gangs and crime go hand-in-hand. Where crime rates are unusually high there could be gangs operating in the area.

Poor School/Community Links

Schools can't be expected to solve the problems of gang involvement alone. Communities with a multi-agency approach to intervention are needed.

Lack of Sports and Recreational Facilities

It may seem an excuse when teens moan that they engage in anti-social behaviour because there is 'nothing to do.' However, where parks and sports facilities give way to housing and commercial interests, there is more than a grain of truth in that statement.

Transient Population

Where people are always coming and going, a neighbourhood can lack a sense of community. A strong community acts as a safeguard against gangs.

Lack of Youth Employment Opportunities

Gangs offer a way to make money and gain status for those young people who feel trapped in unemployment or dead-end jobs.

Youth are Ignored

If youth drug and alcohol abuse go unchecked and young people are treated as a source of problems rather than solutions, a community practically opens the door to gangs.

School Indicators

Rather than safeguarding children from gangs, some schools actually increase the risks by providing an unsupportive environment. We cannot ignore the fact that sooner or later, if nothing is done to tackle it, this new culture of gang glorification will dominate schools and the prison system.

Low Teacher Expectations

Most teachers want the best for their students and work hard to help them overcome difficulties. But if support for the teachers themselves is lacking, performance and morale can drop, and teachers may lose hope.

Conflict Between Home/School Cultures

Schools and families need to work as a team to parent young people. This relationship can break down with families and schools fighting each other over issues such as truancy, behaviour and attitude to work. This makes it harder to protect children from gangs.

Lack of Educational Options

Not all young people are cut out for academic achievement. A good school system will provide alternative routes to success.

Disruptive School Environment

Children need to feel safe and secure while at school. Sadly, some school environments play into the hands of gang recruiters by failing to act on bullying and violence. Pupils are offered a safe haven within a gang where their 'boys' will look out for them.

Lack of Student Participation

In most schools, children are encouraged to participate fully in their education and in other school activities. The more self-worth a child can build up in school, the less likely they will need to seek it outside from gangs.

Lack of Effective Attendance System.

The government have cracked down on school attendance in recent years and this is less of a problem than in the past. With their responsible peers in school, children who regularly play truant will be more likely to hook up with gang members.

Lack of Effective Discipline System

Discipline is a difficult issue for all schools with the need to strike a balance between the 'carrot' and 'stick' approach. A zero-tolerance approach will do little to tackle underlying issues while too much positive attention for troublemakers can reward misbehaviour and deny other children the care they need. What is clear is that we can't start accepting the carrying of weapons into school as the new norm.

Gang Style Clothing and Accessories

Learning about the gang fashions in your area can help teachers to spot the signs of gang affiliation.

CHAPTER 13: The Local Postcode Trap

Being born into or growing up in a 'bad' neighbourhood doesn't mean that a child will become a gang member, but it does add a strong risk factor.

The postcode trap can also immediately put you on the wrong side of an established gang as my own experiences revealed:

On a Saturday evening, I would usually meet up with my older friend. His gang or crew of friends would usually meet up and decide what party or rave they would attend as any young person would do.

The only difference was that this group of young men I was being introduced to were heavily respected gang members from east and south London with a reputation for violent retaliation if disrespected.

That evening we drove to a house party in Tottenham, north London. Deep down in my heart, I knew I shouldn't be hanging around with guys like this but when you're a teenager it was enticing and gave me the reputation that I was connected.

Within minutes of arrival, we were greeted with aggressive hostility and an argument broke out involving one of the older gang members; for the first time, I experienced the feeling that I could lose my life if this situation turned pear-shaped.

As I stood closer to listen cautiously to the argument, I realised it was simply about which area we were from. I was totally perplexed. This young gang member from Tottenham took offence because he thought one of the members of the group was from Hackney.

To my surprise, my friend went back to the car and armed all of the members of the groups with knives and they plotted to attack this young man. They felt he violated them by asking them such questions.

I knew that, if they used these knives, there would be a murder case, possibly a death by retaliation from the other gang and possibly a hefty prison sentence just by being affiliated with this group. In desperation and after pleading and trying to reason with my older friend, we decided to leave. To our disbelief, one member of the other gang followed us on a moped and pulled out a gun, ready to shoot at our car before we sped off.

That was the game changer for me. It left me in a place of anger; that someone could easily take my life over the postcode I was from. It also created paranoia and anxiety and forced me to enter defence mode for many months.

At night, I found myself sleeping with a knife under my pillow to get a good night's sleep. I began to imagine a fearful scenario that because they knew my face, at some point, there would be a home invasion. This wasn't the case and I learned later in life that I had been suffering from post-traumatic stress syndrome from the incident. Prior to this incident, I was naive to think that things of this nature never happened. This made me wake up to the realities of gang violence. Sometimes when you live in an area, you become desensitised to the crime and youth gang problem in the area – that is until you become a victim of it yourself.

Case Study: Being in the Wrong Place

While writing this book, another young boy has just lost his life before it has even started. Once again, it seems to have been a case of him being caught up in a gang turf war – being in the wrong postcode and talking to the wrong people at the wrong time.

19 year-old Kelvin Odunuyi, another rapper, known by the names Dipdat and Lampz was shot outside a Vue cinema in Wood Green, near Tottenham. One of two masked men opened fire from a moped before fleeing the scene.

Fearful of the gang situation in Wood Green, Kelvin's family had moved to Harrow but, despite his mother's warning not to visit his Wood Green friends, he made the fateful decision to disregard the advice.

Police arrested a 21-year-old man on suspicion of murder two days later.

There is also a postcode trap in the sense that people with an address associated with a high crime rate may be treated with suspicion by employers and the authorities. This can affect their job prospects and self-worth.

These are, as we discussed in the previous chapter, both powerful individual risk factors for gang membership. There is also likely to be a strong gang presence in such areas, eagerly looking to recruit these disaffected youths.

With fewer positive social networks to draw on, social mobility is lower in these neighbourhoods. People become stuck in a cycle of poverty.

The Vicious Circle of Postcode, Reputation and Crime Rate

Another effect of the local postcode trap is to make the area less affordable for everyone. This both deepens the level of deprivation and keeps less vulnerable people (by which I mean those who want to live peacefully in a community) from moving into the area.

Take the example of Moss Side, an inner-city area south of Manchester city centre. Moss Side developed a notorious reputation over the 70s and 80s when social deprivation in the area led to a rise in gangs and associated turf wars. Combined with a trade in illegal guns, the results were predictably tragic for those involved and for the reputation of the area. Over time, Moss Side developed a reputation as a 'bad' neighbourhood.

In her blog post, 'Moss Side's Views Have Changed - Have Yours?' (based on a successful local initiative of the same name) Baptist minister Catriona reveals how the cost of her car and house insurance were 'astronomical,' when she lived there. This not only made economic survival tougher for her and other young people trying to get on in life, but it also reduced the appeal of the area further.

With few moderating influences, gangs can gain a firmer foothold and can also offer a way out of poverty through drug-dealing and other criminal pursuits. As the blogger points out, the facts of an individual case (in this case, the gang-related murder of young Jesse James), are overlooked by the media (whether intentionally or through incompetent reporting) in order to further denigrate the name of a well-known 'bad area.'

This not only tightens the postcode trap, but it plays into the Moss Side gangs' hands by adding to the reputation that they want to portray.

Escaping the Postcode Trap

Escaping the postcode trap is not easy but the story of Moss Side (and nearby Hulme) offer a glimpse of a way forward. A huge joint effort from local authorities and the community in the early part of the Noughties led to significant improvements in facilities with new road links built and properties refurbished.

This progress attracted much more positive attention from the media and, while still unable to completely shake its notoriety, Moss Side is no longer regarded as negatively as it was a couple of decades ago.

Case Study: Kurt's Story

The issue of the postcode trap was covered in a 2005 Panorama documentary, 'What Future for Kurt?' Kurt, at the time of the programme, was a seven-year-old boy living in an estate in Rowner, an area of Gosport, Hampshire, known for its high-rise tower blocks. The family talk about the local Rowner Crew gang and the temptations and corrupting influences around them, of how many children were 'sucked in' to a 'whirlpool' of poverty, crime and low aspiration.

There are also interviews with former gang members who talk of the problems of gaining employment with a criminal record and of growing up with only junkies and criminals as role models.

Despite both parents working, Kurt's family were struggling to make ends meet and lumbered with debt. But they were determined not to allow Kurt to become a victim of the postcode trap. Kurt's is a particularly good example of the trap since Rowner, one of the five most deprived parts of the country, has the postcode 'PO13 8,' while nearby Alverstoke, with the postcode 'PO12 2,' is one of the five least deprived. The documentary revealed that people in Rowner were seven times more likely to be on social security than those in Alverstoke.

Kurt's father, Mark, also pointed out his perception of the negative attitude employers had to the area. Says Mark: “Rowner gets mentioned in a job interview and suddenly you've gone from being a possible candidate to a Rowner boy, a Rowner man, one of them, one of them that lives in Rowner.”

Fortunately for Kurt, his parents had managed to stay together, stay in work and had aspirations for him. Hopefully that was enough to rescue him from the lure of gangs.

CHAPTER 14: Joint Enterprise & The Law

Joint Enterprise Prosecutions and Gang Databases

Joint enterprise (JE) is a controversial scheme aimed (at least by those who promote it) at cracking down on gang-related crimes.

JE legislation aims to identify individuals who are linked to gangs and to help and encourage them to change their lifestyle. It also aims to make it easier for prosecutors to charge gang members who are present but non-active when a gang-related crime takes place.

The police maintain several gang databases to help store the gang affiliations of individuals to help with JE programmes and prosecutions.

However, critics argue that the concept of joint enterprise makes it too easy for the authorities to discriminate against certain groups, for example on racial lines.

The Problem with JE Convictions

JE has been the subject of fierce debate with supporters claiming it a necessary tool in the fight against gangs and critics arguing that it criminalises members of certain communities and therefore creates more victims.

Some people charged under the JE legislation have claimed that they were unaware of its existence. They understandably feel unjustly treated when convicted of a gang-related attack despite forensic and witness testimony pointing that they had no physical involvement it.

I saw young people arrested for crimes on Joint Enterprise crimes which they weren't even involved in. I even saw a friend serve eight years in jail for a gang-affiliated robbery. On the day of his release he was deported out of the country, forever separated from his family, children and friends.

Case Study: Michael Christie's JE conviction

Michael Christie was one of six black men convicted of murder and attempted murder in December 2005 under JE legislation. 24-year old doorman Ishfaq Ahmed had been shot and killed a year earlier as he attempted to stop the nightclub he was protecting from being burgled.

Ahmed had tried to stop a group of 11 men forcing their way via a side door into the nightclub where he worked. No gun was ever recovered, and the identity of the killer could not be proven.

During the case, the prosecution linked the defendants to the 'Johnson Crew,' an alleged Birmingham gang, via a two-year old tattoo on one of their chests (the defendant admitted the tattoo represented the gang).

They also linked the defendants to one other using evidence of mobile phone contact (and Christie's admitted connection to one of them).
Although Christie and two other defendants were proven to be in the area, CCTV footage was poor and there was no eye witness identification. However, a police

officer who had been in charge of supervising Christie after his release from a previous sentence, did positively identify him from the CCTV images.

Based on this evidence and the confrontational behaviour of the group when challenged (which indicated to the jury that none of the group could have been unaware that guns were being carried and likely to be used), all six men were sentenced to 30 years on one count of murder and three of attempted murder.

A Centre for Crime and Justice Studies report produced in 2016, 'Dangerous Associations: Joint Enterprise, Gangs and Racism,' asked the question: – 'To what extent do 'gang' discourses influence the process of criminalisation of young black men?'

The report studied two elements: the relationship between the 'gang' and those convicted of serious youth violence and how the 'gangs' discourse was used in the process of prosecution within JE cases.

Here Are Some of the Report's Findings:

- ✓ There was a disproportionally high representation of BAME (Black, Asian and minority ethnic) 'gang nominals' on the three Police databases used. In Manchester, 89 per cent of recorded gang members were BAME individuals despite them forming just a third of the city's make-up. The statistics showed a similar trend in London and Birmingham.
- ✓ In Manchester and London, the small proportion of alleged gang members among young white men was in contrast to their high representation as violent offenders.

- ✓ By separating out black men into different ethnic categories (black Caribbean, black mixed race, black British, etc.) there was an even starker disproportionately high proportion of gang members.
- ✓ Despite forming 18 per cent of the JE prisoner population, BAME individuals formed over 51 per cent of the questionnaire respondents (the questionnaire was titled, Joint Enterprise Not Guilty by Association (JENGbA).
- ✓ In JE cases, due to imprecise academic definitions, the prosecution strategy focused on using common-sense, stereotyped and racialized definitions to create a 'gang discourse' which acted as a signifier to the juries (regardless of whether, as in the Christie case, the judge asked for the evidence to be set aside).
- ✓ The average number of defendants in a JE case was four although one case saw 26 people charged.
- ✓ 59 per cent of the prisoners confirmed that thc 'gangs' discourse was used in their trial. The 'gangs' discourse was significantly more likely to be used in cases involving BAME JE defendants than in those involving white defendants.
- ✓ Most BAME prisoners denied their involvement with co-defendants amounted to being in a gang.
- ✓ BAME prisoners were serving longer average sentences than other prisoners.
- ✓ Nearly half of JE prisoners denied having been at the scene of the crime. The prosecution used a wide range of strategies to place defendants at the scene due to the importance of foresight (i.e. knowledge of the crime which was about to happen) in proving JE cases.
- ✓ The questionnaires returned sometimes revealed no previous contact

between or knowledge of co-defendants.

- ✓ There were key differences in mechanisms used by prosecutors in BAME JE cases including greater use of cell site evidence and reference to music lyrics.

Thinking Point: Gangs and JE

Do you think joint enterprise is a good idea? What are the benefits of punishing all gang members equally for crimes committed by individuals? What are the risks?

Imagine you are in a gang and you receive a letter from the Police warning you to change your lifestyle. How would you feel? What if you were friends with someone in a gang but not actually in the gang?

Activities: Gangs and Ethnicity

Discuss this!

The above report highlights how young black prisoners and ethnic minorities are more often labelled as gang members in Manchester, Nottingham and London.

- ✓ Do you think this a real reflection of gang make-up in the UK or does the JE tool discriminate against BAME groups?
- ✓ Are there any other explanations for the report's findings?

CHAPTER 15: A Guide to Gang Prevention

For parents, this could be the most important chapter of the book.

Protecting our young people from becoming involved with gangs requires awareness of what gangs are, how they operate and the wider gang culture. It also requires positive action to empower our youths to make healthy choices.

Although I've touched on some of the gang prevention approaches currently used in some areas, the book has so far focused on raising awareness.

This chapter looks specifically at what you can do – as a parent, teacher or community member – to help youths protect themselves from being drawn into a life of crime and pain.

Your Children Are at Risk

For parents with existing concerns about their child's behaviour and the influence of local gangs, this section heading will come as no surprise. Other parents may deny that there is any chance their child could get hooked by a gang.

It is important to know that they are wrong. Any child can potentially be targeted by gangs. Whether they push the membership button, the material wealth button or the threat button, gangs are adept at probing for a child's weakness and creating a dependency.

Of course, some children are more at risk than others but starting from the assumption that your child is at risk is the safest option.

Activities: What Are Your (Or Your Child's) Buttons?

Discuss this!

- ✓ Imagine a gang member wants you (or your son or daughter) to deliver a small package to a friend for them. What tactics are most likely to succeed?
- ✓ Could you be bribed with a brand-new pair of £150 Nikes?
- ✓ Would you do it as a 'favour' for an elder you look up to?
- ✓ How would you react if they told you that your parents, brother or sister will get hurt if you don't do this one small thing for them?

Try this!

Gaming chatrooms and mobile phone apps are channels through which gang members could target new recruits. Allowing young people to play games and chat in secret is a big risk, especially when the risk of gangs is high in your area.

1. Schools are advised to set up an online awareness workshop and communicate regularly with parents about online safety.
2. Parents should talk to their children about their online activity. Be particularly aware of any new online friends or the appearance of brand new games or computer equipment in the home.
3. Remind your children that they can talk to you about anything and that

you won't blame them for speaking to strangers or being exposed to inappropriate content.

How to Build Resilience Through Social Skills

Parents may feel powerless to tackle youth street gangs but the truth is that they may have more power than anybody else. The work begins in the home with parents teaching:

Honest and Open Communication

No family ever communicates perfectly but some struggle more than others. Where children or teenagers feel unable to express their emotions, these get bottled up inside.

A gang thrives on repressed feelings because these can be used to fuel antisocial and criminal behaviour. Meanwhile, the gang purports to understand and support the struggling youth.

No emotions are bad. Children need to be allowed to express their feelings of anger, joy, love and fear without being ridiculed or told off. The word 'emote' means to 'move out.' Parents need to help their children to move their emotions out rather than hold on to them.

The pain of unexpressed emotions can be used by gangs as a weapon against society.

Co-operation and Negotiation

Parents need to train their children to co-operate and negotiate with one another. To do this, children need to learn to wear the shoes of someone else. They will then see their point of view and this will help them to work out compromises. This can be tough (even for adults) so be sure to praise your kids when they get it right.

Taking Personal Responsibility

The ability to take responsibility for their choices is one of the greatest gifts a parent can give to their child. It will make them resistant not only to gangs but to making bad life decisions in general.

The Difference between Making the Right Choice and Taking Responsibility

Nobody can make the right choice every time but as long as they are taking ownership of a wrong choice and learning from it, they will be less likely to repeat those mistakes.

Decision-making Skills

Making decisions and taking responsibility for the outcome go hand-in-hand. Socially healthy young people master both and become future leaders.

Some parents tell their children what to do in every situation and they may equate this approach to good, disciplined parenting. However, there is a danger that the child will stop trying to make decisions and become one of life's followers.

Gangs love recruiting followers because they will obediently follow orders with minimal friction. Start helping your child to become a decision-maker by asking their opinions, listening to their views and giving them the chance to come up with their own solutions to problems.

Unconditional Love

Love is a powerful protective force in society. A child who feels loved will be less likely to crave acceptance from a gang or to disrespect themselves by being antisocial. Performance in school, while important, should not be allowed to overshadow a parent's love and respect for their child. Although parents somtimes need to pull up on a bad attitude or bad behaviour, they should never criticise a child for who they are.

Activities: Criticising Behaviour and Not the Child

Try this!

Saying the right thing, especially in the heat of the moment, can be hard for parents. Cast your mind back to a recent fight you had with your child. Did you criticise them or their behaviour? How could you have rephrased things to show your unconditional love?

Example: Your child comes out of a test with an F grade

- Response 1) 'That is pathetic. Are you stupid or just lazy? At this rate you will end up on the scrap heap. I never want to see an F again, you hear me?

What the child internalises: I'm pathetic, stupid, lazy and destined to fail. I am only loved when I do well at school.

- Response 2) 'I'm not going to lie, I'm disappointed. However, I know you want to do well so how can I help? Do you need extra help at school or do you think we need to cut down on some video game time? I'm sure you'll do better next time.

What the child internalises: I'm motivated and capable. I may need some help with this topic (or with prioritising my homework) but under it all my parents love, support and have confidence in me.

Don't beat yourself up about poor communication in the past. It is never too late to change the way you deal with things as a family. However, changing habits is never straightforward; you will have to work to improve your communication skills.

Community Involvement

Studies have shown that young people often feel undervalued or excluded from their communities. Encourage your children to get involved by joining music groups, sports clubs, community-focused interest groups or voluntary organisations. Be prepared to attend with them if they are unconfident at first.

The more connected a young person is with the wider community, the less likely they will want to do harm to it. By connecting with other parents and group members you will also have more people looking out for your child's welfare.

Plan family and one-to-one time. It can be tough to balance work, school, housework and meals, especially for a single parent. Don't let your children become strangers to you.

Keep bonds strong by eating and playing together, sharing family traditions and keeping communication channels open. If you have several children, be sure to set one-to-one time with each of them at least once a week.

If there is family tension, organise a family meeting to talk openly about each other's needs and feelings.

Dealing with peer pressure. Help your children to recognise and come up with simple ways to respond to pressure from friends.

Activities: Dealing with Peer Pressure

Try this!

This could be turned into a fun game for the whole family (you can tailor questions to be age appropriate). Each person in turn can come up with a question a peer might ask, and the others could discuss what a good response would be.

Example question: How would you respond if a peer said, 'If you were a real friend, you would come with me to the fight this afternoon and back me up.'

Example answer: 'If you were a real friend you would listen when I say don't get involved.'

Even very young primary school age children can have fun and learn protective strategies at the same time – it is never too early to start!

It is also a good idea to get to know your children's friends and their parents. Children are often led into gangs or antisocial behaviour through their friends so keeping a close eye on their networks is a wise move.

Set Boundaries

Real discipline is not aggressive or abusive. It is about negotiating reasonable boundaries with your children and setting out the consequences for stepping over them. Once agreed, these boundaries should be stuck to and punishments applied as agreed. This will help children to take responsibility for their decisions.

Gang Awareness

Look through this book with your children. Engage in the highlighted activities. Relate the content to your local area and ask them about experiences they and their friends may have had with gangs.

If your children dress in gang-style clothing, ask what they find appealing about that.

Media Awareness

Point out the glamorisation of gangs on TV, in movies and in music. Make your children aware that a single act of violence can kill and that a person won't necessarily get up after a beating. Encourage them to watch mainstream TV as well as specialised content (mainstream TV provides less positive messages about gangs). When they are old enough, show them more realistic documentaries about gangs.

Getting Started

It doesn't matter how bad your relationship with your children has been up to this point. You can change things at any time.

Even making a small step by introducing one or two of the above approaches into your family routine is a great start and will reduce the likelihood of your child getting into or staying with a gang.

And one less recruit is one less gang member in your community. Multiply that by the number of parents in your community and how does the gang problem look now? More manageable?

Activities: Parent Support Groups

Discuss this!

If the above has inspired you, consider clubbing together with other parents in the area to support one another, share what works and look out for each other's kids.

A strong community is at the heart of all gang prevention strategies. If your area lacks one, help create it from the ground up.

CHAPTER 16: Assessing Gang Threat to Community

Have you ever wondered how much of a problem your community has with gangs and how it compares with other areas? To help establish a perspective on gang activity in your neighbourhood, the following four level model can be used.

It gives suggestions for interventions depending on the level of gang activity suspected and has been adapted from the one presented by the Department of Justice in Canada in their publication: 'Gang Prevention: A Resource Guide on Youth & Gangs.'

Level 1: No Gangs

In these neighbourhoods there are no signs of any gang existence at all. Nevertheless, wherever there are disaffected youths there is always the risk of gangs forming so it is important for communities not to become complacent.

Interventions at this level would be best focused on:

- ✓ Teaching parenting skills.
- ✓ Reinforcing positive messages around home, family and community.
- ✓ Building or maintaining strong connections between parents, schools and the wider community.
- ✓ Teaching multi-cultural sensitivity, awareness, tolerance and respect.
- ✓ Reinforcing attendance, discipline and a sensible dress code in schools.

Level 2: Early Gangs

Here, some or all members of the community are aware of the existence of gangs but these have either not been publicly recognised or they are regarded as little more than a nuisance.

In this situation, communities should consider:

- ✓ Working with the police and community organisations on sharing information and developing gang awareness programmes.
- ✓ Running gang awareness and prevention programmes in schools and the community.
- ✓ Improving community sports facilities and activity programmes.
- ✓ Cracking down on vandalism and graffiti.
- ✓ Launching public information campaigns on the threat of gangs.

Level 3: Active Gangs

In such communities, gangs are a visible and increasing threat. Residents will mostly be aware of their existence and be concerned about it. To avoid becoming dominated by gangs, communities might:

- ✓ Establish parent education programmes
- ✓ Develop strategies aimed at suppressing gangs and/or targeting specific problem areas.
- ✓ Mobilise themselves to take proactive measures.
- ✓ Improve employment prospects for young people.

- ✓ Develop multi-agency organisations to share information and co-ordinate interventions.

Level 4: Gang Dominance

In these neighbourhoods, gangs have established themselves so deeply that most, if not all, young people will be actively approached by gang members. Where gangs hold sway, young people (and adults) will often fear to speak out against the problem due to the threat of retaliation.

To improve the situation in gang-dominated areas, communities can:

- ✓ Continue to mobilise as a community. This is their greatest asset.
- ✓ Form strong partnerships between community organisation and law enforcement professionals including, where possible, gang experts.
- ✓ Launch campaigns to reclaim public areas (parks, streets, etc.) from the scourge of gangs.

CHAPTER 17: Rules for Working with Gangs

Choosing to work in the community to work with gangs and disrupt their development is a fantastic way to help young people and heal communities. However, people need to walk into this task with their eyes open. They should be prepared to meet a negative, confrontational attitude – at least in the beginning – and this can be difficult barrier to overcome.

Remember the 'Three Rs'

As explained in an earlier chapter, respect is of central importance to a gang member and the gang as a whole. If a young person you are working or communicating with feels that you are disrespecting him or her – or the gang itself – they will, at the very least, refuse to co-operate any further. You must find ways to develop mutual respect relationships if you hope to have a positive effect on gang activity.

Basic Guidelines

Here are some broad guidelines for handling gang member relations:

- ✓ **Set firm ground rules.** Showing respect for a gang member does not mean letting them call all the shots and agreeing with everything he or she says and does. Agree on some ground rules from the outset (e.g. meeting at a certain place and time, not carrying weapons or drugs, being alone or with one friend, etc.) Stick to your side of the agreement but remind them that you expect them to show you similar respect by following through on their agreements. Framing situations in terms of respect is an effective technique to manage these situations. If you are too lenient with a gang member, they will usually take advantage by pushing more and more boundaries. The more they seem in control of the relationship, the more respect they will earn from the gang, so it is important to work hard to achieve an equal power balance.

✓ **Don't use intimidation or scare tactics**. Strategies aimed at using fear or force as a deterrent tend to be ineffective at best and can even be dangerous. Young people who are affiliating with a gang will usually be far more afraid of upsetting the older gang members than they will be of anything you can threaten them with. Prison is hardly a deterrent. In some areas, so many of a young person's fellow crew are behind bars or in institutions that a prison sentence creates a chance to reunite. In any case, a spell inside is seen as a boost to their reputation which will go down well with the gang. Add to this the fact that negative experiences in the family, school and community will have often created a hostility and immunity to authority figures and it is clear to see how scare tactics don't work. Actual intimidation of gang members can even have dangerous repercussions as they might escalate into violent conflict there and then or retribution in the future.

✓ **Use media attention wisely**. Gang members will often want to use media coverage as a means to enhance their reputation. To appear in the newspaper, on radio or, best of all, on TV gives gangs the chance to display their presence, show off their signs and symbols and to emphasise their power by wearing expensive jewellery, driving flash cars and even brandishing weapons. This can easily turn media attention into a means to glorify gangs so it is important for you to control the process by communicating clearly with the media (and being selective on which media you speak to). Your aim should be that the negative aspects of gang involvement (arrest, conviction, death, etc.) come out more strongly than anything else.

- ✓ **Don't lose the individual**. By treating young people as individuals, you can show your respect for them as a person. Treating them as simply a 'gang member' or 'troubled youth' can encourage 'wannabes' to join gangs or push young gang recruits into deeper affiliation. This is an example of a psychological process known as 'projective identification': the more you treat someone as a certain kind of person, the more likely they will be to become that sort of person.

- ✓ **Prevent conflict as much as possible**. Gang culture, conflict and violence are deeply entwined. When working with gangs, it is easy to say or do something which creates hostility or anger. Be aware of the signs and de-escalate the situation as much as possible. Communication skills are critical here. If a gang member criticises you for disrespecting them, phrases like, "I'm sorry you feel I'm disrespecting you. I didn't mean what I said to come out that way," can be very useful tools in calming things down. Allowing or encouraging bad feelings to get out of hand will usually lead to some sort of vengeance or retaliation, from the affronted member or the gang as a whole.

- ✓ **Be an individual**. A typical gang member will have a negative attitude towards anyone or anything that represents authority. Be prepared to approach gang members as an individual and a fellow human being rather than a group representative (especially if your group is related to law enforcement).

- ✓ **Be vigilant at all times**. Never be caught off your guard when working with a gang member. Be aware of who and what is around you at all times. If you are transporting a gang member across town, be mindful of which gang's territory you are in. Showing up in a rival's territory can be dangerous for both your client and yourself.

- ✓ **Be careful of being played**. Be aware that a gang member's intention to work with you may have an ulterior motive. For example, if you are asked to drop them off at a certain place and pick them up again ten minutes later, you could unwittingly be playing the role of a drugs carrier. If you are working in an official capacity (e.g. as a counsellor), your client may ask you for advice and then report you when there are negative consequences after they follow it (e.g. missing a curfew).

- ✓ **Leave on good terms**. A young gang member who feels you have it in for them are unlikely to benefit from your interaction and may even seek to retaliate for perceived disrespect. Even if the meeting hasn't been the success you hoped for, make sure that there is no bad blood between you before you go your separate ways.

CHAPTER 18: Working with Families

It takes a special kind of person to work effectively with gang members and it is not for the faint-hearted.

However, working with families and young people who are not (yet) gang members, while also challenging, may be a more realistic route for most people interested in tackling gangs.

This kind of community work can be even more important than working with existing gangs as it helps to prevent the development of the local gangs. It can also be a powerful source of support for families and youths in difficult circumstances.

Basic Guidelines

Here are some broad guidelines for working with families in neighbourhoods troubled by gangs:

- ✓ **Practise effective listening**. As well as listening carefully to the words family members and young people are using, be aware of other clues (body language, tone of voice, etc.) Pay attention also to the interactions between family members for clues about their underlying relationships.

- ✓ **Avoid blaming**. Family circumstances can be difficult and no one can fairly judge parents and other family members without walking in their shoes. For example, understand that many mothers in gang-dominated areas will be ambivalent about their child carrying a knife. While they may discourage and warn their children about the consequences, they will also know about situations where unarmed children have been killed while another child has avoided an attack because they or their friends could show they had a weapon. In any case, blaming (including self-blame) is rooted in the past. It is far more constructive to focus the conversations on the present and how positive actions now can lead to a better future for the family and community as a whole. This will help to enlist family members as allies and encourage and empower them to make a positive difference.

✓ **Make yourself available.** Being available means being open emotionally as well as contactable. When working with families and at-risk youths, you may be the only source of support they have. Although you can't be at their beck and call 24/7, the easier it is for families to contact you, the better your relationship with them will be. When engaged in conversation with family members, try to adopt a relaxed pose and give them your full attention without making judgements. A sympathetic ear can be a huge source of comfort for families under pressure.

✓ **Deal only in facts**. It is easy to be drawn into taking sides when connecting with families. Some families will turn rumours and opinions into facts which they then use to justify their actions (or inaction). While acknowledging their perspective, it is important to remain detached and to make points based on established facts.

- ✓ **Help families to help themselves**. Depending on your role (friend, social worker, teacher, etc.) families may lean on you to act on their behalf. Where possible, encourage them to take the actions themselves. Empowering families in this way is far more useful and rewarding in the long run than being a crutch.

- ✓ **Share knowledge**. Although emotional and practical support is valuable, accurate information on how to access other forms of help are equally important. Some families are simply unaware of what resources are out there for them or are confused about who best to contact. In addition to general sources of support, draw upon specific resources which you are familiar with as part of your role (e.g. a police officer will have knowledge of legal procedures, a nurse will know what health and social services are available and a mum will have experience of local activities and support services).

- ✓ **Be sensitive to family differences**. Family norms vary widely. Differences in cultural background, religion, social class, region and support networks will affect how the families and young people you work with view and work with you. By treating everyone with respect and refusing to judge, you will usually find the family opening up to you over time. Some family members may be less open to working with you than others and you may even experience some hostility. As mentioned earlier in this book, some gangs have such an insidious effect on a community that non-gang members pick up and embrace the mentality to a degree. They may side with one gang over another and become defensive when that gang is criticized. Some families may be unwilling to co-operate due to fear of retaliation from gangs. They may have already experienced violence or threats from gangs and may have been warned not to 'snitch.'

- ✓ **Avoid patronising families**. There are few things guaranteed to turn a family against you than an attitude of superiority. There is a fine line between providing advice and guidance and insulting a family member's intelligence. If a family has lived in an area troubled by gangs for a long time, they will most probably know a lot more about how gangs operate than an outsider, no matter how much academic knowledge you have.

- ✓ **Report child abuse.** We all have a responsibility to report suspected child abuse. If you are working as part of an organisation, familiarise yourself with safeguarding procedures and policies as necessary. If you are not part of an organisation, you can call the NSPCC on 0808 800 5000 if you have any concerns.

- ✓ **Know your limits.** Working with gang members and their families can be emotionally exhausting, especially if your efforts are achieving few results. Be aware of your own physical and mental wellbeing and make sure you have someone to talk to if things get too much. Don't be ashamed if you have to admit defeat sometimes; no one can end gang violence on their own.

Generational Gang Families

Some families will actively support the activities of a gang because they have a previous or ongoing family connection with it. In such cases, it can be difficult to separate the gangs out from the wider family network.

Having older family members with gang connections is a big risk factor for young people. Working with generational gang families can be very challenging but particularly rewarding if a long-established gang chooses a different road.

Generational gangs will almost certainly have experienced family tragedies, so it is important to handle them with respect and sensitivity.

Effects on Non-Gang Affiliated Children

Where gangs are deeply-rooted in a community, it is not only the families and victims of crime that suffer. Here are some of the worries that students in troubled neighbourhoods may have:

- ✓ Gang disruption at school.
- ✓ Encountering gang members on the way to and from school.
- ✓ Being targeted by students who are known or believed to be in a gang.
- ✓ Facing peer pressure to join a gang.
- ✓ Being mistaken as a gang member during school or in the street by rival gangs.
- ✓ Presence of firearms and knives at school.
- ✓ Escalating interracial/ethnic tensions at school and in the community.

CHAPTER 19: Community Responses

Gangs are not just a family, school or police problem!

Gangs are a community problem and, as such, require a community response. No one service agency or community group can successfully intervene to stop the development of gangs or prevent gangs from rising up.

Co-operation between multiple agencies: parents, the police, government officials, businesses and others is proving to be the most effective way of dealing with gangs.

These collaborative interventions and prevention programmes are more likely to be effective in communities at the Level 1 and Level 2 stages of gang activity where gangs are virtually non-existent or are only just becoming established.

Prevention is the key to controlling gang activity and everyone in a community can help in the drive to stop our young people from forming gangs or joining existing ones. Effective anti-gang efforts tend to begin with the formation of strong, positive partnerships between parents, schools, law enforcement organisations and religious institutions.

Activities: What can we offer?

Discuss this!

- ✓ Part 1: Go through each of the following groups of people and write down what each might be able to offer when it comes to tackling gangs.

- Parents
- Teachers
- Students
- Police officers
- Religious leaders
- Media
- Other People in The Community

Compare what you have written and discuss your answers.

✓ Part 2: Discuss why you think different kinds of groups working together might be better than one type of group working alone when it comes to dealing with gangs?

Needs Assessment & Staff Recruitment

Two of the most important considerations to make when designing a gang prevention or intervention programme are needs assessment and choosing the right people for the job.

A needs assessment is designed to highlight the gap between the current situation in a community and the desired outcome. Programmes which are designed on the basis of formal needs assessments tend to last longer and produce better outcomes than those which do not come from this process.

This isn't surprising. A programme set up without a clear idea of what its purpose is will be more easily derailed or diverted. Once the needs assessment has been carried out, the next important task is to recruit the right people to carry out the various parts of the programme. This may or may not require a formal recruitment process depending on what type of agency is running the programme.

Needs assessments and personnel selection is as important in law enforcement and school-based interventions as it is with more loosely structured community groups.

Only when the needs assessment has been done and the people put in place should the group or agency begin the programme design. It is important to ensure the aims of the group are realistic given the people delivering the programme on the ground and the resources (e.g. money and time) they have access to. Unrealistic programmes are a source of friction between staff and managers.

Looking after the staff delivering the programme should continue throughout its duration. Staff should be provided with adequate and ongoing training and personal development opportunities; fair and open evaluation and supervision processes; team building experiences and the opportunity to talk through stress and other difficulties.

Prevention Strategies

There is little point in channelling energy and resources into intervention strategies without trying to stop the inflow of youths into the gang system.

It is also the moral and legal duty of civilized societies to safeguard our vulnerable young people. Therefore, prevention strategies must be prioritised (or at least given equal weight).

Primary prevention strategies target the entire population in high-risk areas. Secondary prevention strategies focus on 7 to 14 year-olds deemed at high risk of being recruited as gang members.

School-based prevention strategies need to be age-specific, developmentally appropriate and culturally sensitive. If individuals and agencies (such as 2020 Dreams/Hard 2 Engage) are being brought in to the school environment, they need to be able to provide risk-assessed services and employ DBS-cleared facilitators where appropriate.

The content type of any prevention programme should match the students' level of risk. For example, an awareness workshop aimed at secondary school children in areas where known gangs are operating will need to be much more intense than a similar workshop aimed at early primary school children in areas with only minor gang activity.

The earlier a prevention programme can be delivered, the more success it is likely to have.

Programmes which any school can begin implementing almost straight away include:

- ✓ Internal staff training on gang awareness (this can be provided by 2020 Dreams/Hard 2 Engage).
- ✓ A clear behavioural code.
- ✓ A sensible dress code.
- ✓ Anti-graffiti policy. This should involve understanding the nature of school graffiti (is it produced by gang members, gang wannabes, taggers or street artists) and removing it promptly.
- ✓ Victim support and counselling services (including appropriate referral mechanisms).
- ✓ Visitor screening and robust site entrance security measures.
- ✓ Extra adult presence around communal areas (stairwells, outside bathrooms, etc.)
- ✓ Set up a networking system with parents and the wider community.
- ✓ Use the school website, social media and mobile apps to keep parents informed of your gang prevention activities.
- ✓ Host gang awareness and prevention workshops or classes for parents.
- ✓ Strengthen connections with local police and co-ordinate gang prevention measures.
- ✓ Increase extra-curricular activities to provide more positive outlets for young people.
- ✓ Help build or get involved with existing community activities to integrate students.

Activities: A School Gang Helpline

Discuss this!

- ✓ One of the earliest rules that is drummed into gang members, wherever in the UK they are based, is that 'snitching' is unacceptable. This has led to a culture whereby young children can be killed on a crowded street and nobody comes forward to provide information to the authorities.
- ✓ Consider the merit of a school Gang Helpline. This would be a confidential service enabling a student to speak to someone about what they have witnessed or heard without being outed as a snitch.
- ✓ Think about how such a service could operate in your school. Who would be best placed to operate the service?

School Intervention Strategies

Intervention strategies involve closely working with existing gang members to help them to leave the gang and integrate back into society. If one or more gang members are known to be enrolled in your school, the following intervention programmes can help to reduce problem behaviours from affecting other students:

- ✓ Increase one-to-one supervision of gang affiliated students.
- ✓ Assign an assistant to help monitor class behaviour.
- ✓ Provide parent consultation services for concerned parents.
- ✓ Give teachers specialised training on managing conflict.

CHAPTER 20: Community Organisation & Mobilisation

Working with the wider community can be daunting. After all, there are many different public and private institutions and organisations all with their own people, structures, roles and agendas.

Some of these organisations join forces with others to form collaborations and it is not always easy to understand which groups are responsible for what.

To begin working with the community, it can be helpful to split the process into four parts: research, involvement, co-ordination and mobilisation.

Researching the Community

Set aside some time – alone or as a group – to fill in the blanks when it comes to which agencies are responsible for which aspect of community life. The internet is an amazing resource for this because most organisations and institutions will at least have a website with an 'About Us' section which should reveal where it sits within the wider framework of the community.

Make a note of how organisations are inter-related (drawing this as a tree can help to make sense of the connections), who the important contacts are and whether they are running any projects around gangs at that point in time.

Involving the Community

The next step is to reach out and contact those community groups and agencies which could potentially work with you on tackling the gang problems in your area. Don't forget local citizens themselves. Speak to people in the park or at the shops and enlist their help in whatever capacity they can provide it.

Former gang members can be incredibly useful assets as they have in-depth knowledge of the gang scene and are more likely to make a connection with high risk young people.

Co-ordinating Interventions

Where there are existing or potential intervention programmes in place, think of how your school, organisation or agency can link your interventions into them.

Meetings between agencies can generate brand new ideas or enable both parties to run their programmes more efficiently. Piece by piece you will find that you are helping to build a united, multi-agency task force focused on the aim of reducing the gang threat and reclaiming your community.

Mobilising the Community

There is a big difference between a connected community and a mobilised one. It is possible for communities to create many agency networks yet not achieve results because they are either moving in different directions or not moving at all.

Mobilising a community requires creating a shared goal (i.e. reclaiming the community from the hands of gangs) and generating the passion to move towards it together. A strong 'mission statement' and a list of aims and objectives can help to achieve this.

Mobilisation involves aligning each separate group's agenda with the overall group goal and then creating a strong, emotional connection. It might involve working to alter people's perceptions of the gang threat.

This should be quite easy in a gang-afflicted community. After all, the police want to drive down crime figures; parents want their sons and daughters to grow up in safety; schools want their students to thrive and their pass rates to improve; religious leaders want to help the vulnerable; youth and sports clubs want to increase membership while reducing difficult behaviour. Even private businesses want to attract customers and secure their premises.

Some agencies may need more persuading than others to get on board with a community anti-gang intervention. They may be worried about possible retaliation from gangs should their involvement become public knowledge.

They may also be worried about upsetting certain stakeholders or communities. Mobilisation also needs the group to clarify definitions, open up clear communication channels and agree on specific actions.

By following the four-step process above, the seemingly impossible task of uniting disparate community groups into a unified force, dedicated to driving out gang activity, can be achieved.

The Evolving Community

Communities never stay still for long. New agencies spring up; the government or council introduces new legislation; interventions achieve milestones or hit snags; key personnel move departments or stand down; a factory shuts down or a supermarket springs up.

All of these things affect the community in clear or more hidden ways and this can impact on how effective community gang programmes will be. For example, the arrival of a big employer can suddenly open doors for young people looking for work, giving them a positive future to hold on to and increasing the likelihood of them avoiding joining or leaving a gang.

However, the situation changes, community groups need to adapt to either take advantage of new opportunities or minimise new threats. By keeping an open mind and regularly evaluating the state of the community, group organisers can ensure gang interventions evolve over time and continue to remain relevant.

This is the secret to establishing long-term programmes which deliver real results as opposed to short-sighted 'knee-jerk' reactions which can sometimes cause as many problems as they solve.

Challenges to Gang Prevention Programmes

A strong, community-rooted, multi-agency intervention strategy will increase the chances of positive results but it would be unrealistic not to expect to come across challenges.

Here Are Some of The Main Barriers to Programme Success:

- ✓ Lack of funding.
- ✓ Inadequate training.
- ✓ Recruitment/retention problems.
- ✓ Political interference (national policies conflicting with local initiatives).
- ✓ Conflicts between agencies.
- ✓ Loss of an organisation creating a missing link in the process.
- ✓ Personality clashes.
- ✓ Weak leadership.
- ✓ Poor evaluation processes.
- ✓ Loss of focus on main goal.
- ✓ Corruption (e.g. gang infiltration)

To avoid these issues becoming major problems, there should be regular reviews scheduled. This will give the organisations involved the chance to assess progress, bring up any conflicts (and so nip them in the bud), address any needs for fundraising and find ways around any other obstacles.

It is also a good idea to regularly reinforce the group's 'mission statement' and remind everyone what the overall purpose of coming together as a community is for.

CHAPTER 21: Suppression

Part of any multi-agency efforts to stamp out gangs has to involve a suppression element.

While I believe that preventative programmes in families and schools and social interventions aimed at supporting young gang members to make better decisions are the most effective in disrupting the formation of gangs, they alone are not enough.

Suppression covers the many different strategies aimed at disrupting gang activities and prosecuting gang members.

Formal and Informal Social Control Measures Include:

- ✓ Close supervision and monitoring of gang members by police and related criminal justice agencies. The London Metropolitan Police have a Gang Matrix to provide intelligence on gangs.
- ✓ Gang sweeps whereby a large number of gang members are arrested in one raid.
- ✓ Raids targeting the proceeds of gang activity (e.g. drug busts, seizing illegal weapons, etc.)
- ✓ Community-based interventions (neighbourhood watch, informant networks, etc.)
- ✓ Zero-tolerance school policies (exclusions, expulsions, etc.)
- ✓ Saturation patrols in certain areas with police officers maintaining a highly visible presence.

- ✓ Knife and gun amnesties.
- ✓ Anti-social behaviour deterrents (special kinds of lighting or sound can be used to stop youths congregating around known trouble spots).
- ✓ Aggressive enforcement of curfews.
- ✓ Awarding of ASBOs (anti-social behaviour orders) to deter gang members from entering certain areas.
- ✓ Granting of new legislative powers (i.e. Joint Enterprise convictions).
- ✓ Vertical prosecutions of prominent gang members (see below).

Whereas preventions and social interventions aim to help young people to feel better about themselves, to escape the postcode trap, to make smarter life decisions and to ultimately say 'no' to gangs, suppression aims to clean the streets from gangs.

As such, any potential or active gang member is a valid target in suppression strategies. This is another reason why young gang members should work hard to maintain good relationships with those who are trying to support them.

The use of suppression tactics is unpredictable, and it is much more difficult to help a young person once they are within the criminal justice system.

Vertical Prosecutions

A vertical prosecution is where one investigator is in charge of a case from beginning to end. This offers several advantages over horizontal prosecutions where investigators focus on their speciality.

This is Because:

- The investigator becomes intimately familiar with all facts related to the case.
- There is less risk of the case lacking any critical evidence at trial.
- There is continuity for victims and witnesses.
- Witnesses don't have to repeat evidence as often.
- The investigator will be highly experienced.
- There is less reliance on other people's competence.

Is Suppression Effective?

Despite being the most regularly used tactic in many areas of gang activity, studies seem to show that gang suppression as a primary strategy is the least effective in eradicating gangs, at least in the long-term.

It is worth emphasising again that most of the evidence available points to multi-agency and multi-dimensional approaches to tackling gangs as being associated with the best and most sustainable outcomes.

In addition, because different areas will have a different gang profile and level of gang activity, each approach will have to be tailored to that town, city or neighbourhood.

Suppression can play a powerful role in a combined strategy but there is debate as to how effective measures such as gang sweeps really are in protecting the community.

For example, gang sweeps and JE convictions which seem to target specific ethnic groups might lead to an overall increase in community tensions, acting as fuel for further gang formation.

Another risk is that gang members will simply hide or move weapons, lie low for a while and then emerge, as strong as ever, after the dust settles.

Having said that, the value of suppression should not be entirely dismissed. Some studies suggest that suppression does successfully limit the damage that existing gangs can do and can be particularly effective in tackling the more violent or long-term gang offenders.

Activities: Gang Suppression Tactics

Discuss this!

- ✓ Why do you think suppression measures such as those listed above aren't that effective in tackling gangs?
- ✓ Why do you think many areas still choose to use gang suppression tactics?
- ✓ Do you think that suppression can help in some areas of gang activity?
- ✓ If you were involved in allocating funds to different anti-gang programmes, what proportion would you give to suppression measures and why?

Case study: The Comprehensive Gang Prevention, Intervention and Suppression Model

This model, supported by the federal Office of Juvenile Justice and Delinquency Prevention in America, has been running, in various forms, since 1993.

In the initial years, researchers studied results from five cities, comparing neighbourhoods which had implemented the plan with comparison sites that hadn't.

They found that in the three areas where the model had been properly applied, there was a statistically significant drop in gang violence and, in two of the areas, a corresponding reduction in drug-related offences.

In 2009, another evaluation looked at four cities with very different gang profiles (LA, Richmond, Milwaukee and North Miami Beach). Researchers found that the model had been applied in each case but with different levels of impact. Nevertheless, all areas showed a reduction in one or more crime indicators.

Suppression and Efficiency

Communities have limited funds to spend on dealing with gang problems so every penny must be accounted for. As well as being criticised for their lack of effectiveness, suppression-only programmes are often more expensive than other gang interventions.

When designing any intervention programme, it is important to look at efficiency. How much money is it going to cost? How much money is it going to save? How will it benefit the community in the short-term? What about the long-term?

It is not always easy to tie definite numbers to an intervention but there should be some attempt to quantify efficiency to avoid expensive programmes being rolled out just to be seen to be doing something.

One way of increasing the efficiency of anti-gang programmes is to join forces with the private sector. Businesses may be persuaded to invest in resources in order to attract more customers or reduce the risk to their assets. Thinking outside of the box is the key to improving how we deal with gangs as a community.

Combining roles is another way to make tackling gangs more efficient. For example, police forces could send officers into schools to talk to children about the dangers of gangs, helping to prevent the very problems they are suppressing on the street.

CHAPTER 22: Social Intervention

We all live as part of an interconnected network. Even the most isolated individual will have some other people with whom they interact and often one or two real relationships. In fact, gangs can only influence young people in the long-term by providing some element of social support.

This means that whatever the source of a gang intervention programme: youth-serving agency, school, grassroots group, church, health service, police force or another organisation, there must be a social element for it to be effective.

Here is where some single-agency interventions fall down. For example, a zero-tolerance crackdown on gangs by law enforcement may take youths off the street, but it does nothing to break down their social bonds.

In fact, it usually has the opposite effect with prisons becoming akin to youth clubs and prisoners gaining respect and integrating further with the gang by being inside.

All agencies involved in tackling gangs need to resist the urge to treat young gang members as 'the enemy' and work hard to reach out to the individuals involved.

By maintaining a strong and positive link between young people, their families and the wider community, there is always a way back for the troubled youth.

Building Meaningful Social Relationships

Creating meaningful social relationships in the context of gang intervention means striking a careful balance.

As detailed in earlier chapters, approaching a gang member with an authoritarian or disrespectful attitude will scupper a relationship before it even gets off the ground.

On the other hand, a social intervention has to be about much more than engaging in small talk or providing a listening ear although these things are important too.

A young gang member will have their own agenda which may include offloading emotional problems, earning the respect of the gang, scaring off the authorities, making money or a combination of these motivations.

Staff who are too passive will allow the gang member to push their agenda and control the interaction. No lasting social relationship will be created in such circumstances, the staff member will be regarded with contempt and the intervention will fail.

To avoid this outcome, all staff involved in an intervention need to be clear about what their agenda is for the interaction.

It is not about 'fixing' a young gang member but about reinforcing their positive behaviours and helping them to take certain steps that will cause them to drift away from the gang and gang culture as they mature.

There are many different tools and models that can be used to make this task easier. The following model highlights three overall aims that can be used to guide each interaction with a young gang recruit: positive communication, social development and social control.

Positive Communication

It is easier to persuade a young gang member to maintain a relationship with you if they leave each interaction feeling better about themselves than before they arrived.

Despite any apparent bravado, gang members are usually suffering from chronic low self-esteem. At first, they are likely to be very defensive, convinced that you are there to remind them about all the mistakes they have made and how bad or worthless they are.

By refusing to criticise them as a person and by treating them with respect, they will be more likely to relax and open up, perhaps admitting to some of the bad things they have done.

A good tactic to avoid blame and focus on solutions is to bring the conversation back to the present and the future.

Activities: From Past to Present

Try this!

Turning conversations from the past to the present is easier the more you practice it. Come up with a way to switch these three sentences from past focus to present focus:

1. I've done some really bad things in my life; things that you wouldn't believe!
2. Drugs is all I know. My grandad did drugs, my dad did drugs and my mum, she even did drugs.
3. I can't get anything right at school. Teachers know I'm trouble and they don't even bother with me anymore.

For example, for Sentence 1 you might say, "That was in the past and can't be changed. Let's talk about the person you are now and what you can do to make your life better." Note, you are not making judgements about their past or condoning it. You are simply encouraging them to move on.

Feel free to change the example sentences or add your own.

If a young person leaves a meeting with you feeling that you have treated them with respect, listened to them and accepted them as a human being they will associate your intervention with a good experience and be more likely to want to come back.

The problem is that most people involved in a gang are street-smart. Being involved in a gang, carrying weapons and fearing for your life makes your cognitive senses more alert. You need to be aware of rival gangs, police, or anything that could harm you. So, gang members are fully aware of the repercussions of their actions, and to a certain extent I don't believe they care.

I don't believe the approach is to patronise youths but to show them the harsh realities of their choices and also to make them aware that making the right choices is easier than they think.

Social Development

While they are acting as a gang member, a young person's social development stalls. Rejected by society, they will hide their pain within and use it as justification for their anger and violent behaviour. The deeper they integrate with the gang, the more their actions will be governed by fear (of the gang and the authorities), anger and often alcohol and drugs.

Any evidence of reflection on their own behaviour, however small, should be taken as a positive sign. This can be used to gently ask further questions about their feelings and motivations. They can also be used to encourage the youth to think about the way other people might feel about their actions and about what lies ahead if they follow the same path.

Encouraging social development can be a slow and frustrating process but if it one day ends with the youth deciding to leave the gang then it will be worth the effort.

Social Control

Social development goes hand-in-hand with social control. The ability to control our behaviour despite strong emotions is one of the characteristics which separates the child from the adult.

Many young gang members are not at heart bad kids. They are just unable to deal constructively with the pain and anger they have internalised. As they learn to trust and open up during their time with you, they are likely to bring up more personal and painful material.

Sometimes this may lead to an angry outburst but at other times they might display restraint. When you praise them for their maturity and control it reinforces this behaviour and increases their ability to keep a cool head.

This, in turn, reduces the likelihood of them committing acts of violence and can even help them to manage their emotions during future job interviews.

Once they have built up a level of social control, the young person will no longer be at the mercy of the gang and may be ready to start integrating back into society in a positive way.

Helping young people to feel better about themselves, promoting their social development and helping them to control their behaviour should be the agenda of all social interventions. Young people will then be able to 'fix' themselves.

CHAPTER 23: Social Opportunities

As well as disrupting gang activity and preventing young people from joining street gangs, communities have to provide our youth with alternative social activities.

These can include a combination of sports and interest groups, community focused organisations and, of course, training and employment opportunities.

Sports and Interest Groups

Sports teams have the ability to offer young people the sense of belonging they are looking for but only if they offer a genuine welcome to people from all backgrounds and actively encourage team-building.

Sports teams which develop into cliques are of no benefit because they reinforce the feelings of exclusion that many young people have felt at school and even within their own families.

In areas where gangs are established, the community must do more than just open up multiple sports facilities. Interventions will need to actively integrate youths into sports and activities they might be interested in.

The 'Changing Course' guide describes this as offering a 'brand' for at-risk children, something that can reflect youth culture and offer a rival to the allure of gang membership.

For example, skateboarding, parkour, music studios and street dancing offer a cool urban style of activity with an element of individual flair and an anti-authoritarian edge.

These activities are also attractive to young people because of their low barrier to entry (providing activity providers keep costs low).

Likewise, activities such as DJing, street art and T-shirt design can help youths to get constructively engaged in the community while reflecting this appealing youth brand.

Having said that, there is nothing to prevent traditionally exclusive sports providers (tennis clubs, cricket clubs, sailing clubs, etc.) from opening their doors and reaching out to the less well-off. This can also act to liven up tired organisations by giving them a fresh source of potential talent.

Of course, a lot of effort will need to go into effectively marketing these activities to troubled youths.

Community-Focused Organisations

Although sports and other interest groups can foster a sense of belonging and help to build self-esteem, participating in organisations which benefit the community as a whole can really transform young gang members and wannabes into responsible citizens.

Encouraging our young people to join voluntary organisations or non-profits working with vulnerable people in society (or serving other just causes) can help them to expand their horizons and even discover a new life purpose (after all, they usually know how it feels to be rejected).

Training and Employment

A lack of youth employment prospects is a key motivator for young people to join gangs. It is difficult for youths from troubled backgrounds, who often suffer from low self-worth, to compete in a weak job market and they may find themselves caught in a postcode trap: rejected by employers due to coming from a 'bad area' and forced to pay higher premiums for insurance as a result of increased crime.

Gangs will often step in to fill the employment gap in such areas. Dealing drugs is one of the most common activities carried out by gang members of all ranks with even the youngest recruits used as carriers and lookouts.

Even where unskilled jobs are available in the community, some young people will prefer the easy gains they can make from drug sales above a low-paying job, especially where there is little prospect of progression and/or working conditions are harsh.

The low employment and crime cycle worsens when young people get convicted of an offence. This makes them even less employable, particularly if they have been convicted of violent crimes.

Where gangs are deeply entrenched, specialised drug gangs might spring up and there may be networks of weapon and people trafficking in operation. In the worst cases, super-gangs become linked with and may even compete with serious criminal organizations.

Here is where business leaders can really make a difference and help in the drive against gangs. They can consider giving people from difficult areas and families a chance and creating real job opportunities in areas of high unemployment.

Attracting businesses to the area is also the job of local councils and even the media can help to lift the reputation of a community out of the gutter.

Case Study: Timpson

Timpson, a national retailer specialising in shoe repairs, key cutting and engraving, are a business which has embraced the concept of equal opportunities. They are prepared to give a chance to ex-offenders and marginalised groups and offer immediate training and development to all staff. On their website, Timpson state, ' We pay our colleagues as much as we can afford rather than as little as we can get away with.'

Businesses such as Timpson offer a way back into the community for young people who have lost their way and are an example of how businesses can play their part in disrupting the vicious cycle of crime and unemployment.

A job (or even better, a career), can motivate a young person to pursue success and fulfilment legally rather than resort to criminal activities. Meaningful employment is also a means for young people to build self-worth, belief in their abilities and take control of their future direction.

Where full employment opportunities are lacking, encouraging youths to take on temporary summer jobs, apprenticeships or internships can help them to overcome personal barriers, build up constructive relationships and demonstrate to future employers that they have a work ethic.

An effective gang intervention programme will look at all options for creating job and training opportunities for young people, drawing on the experience and knowledge of multiple agencies. Where there is an ethnic component to gang formation, people and agencies from those communities may be able to source job opportunities through their contacts and shared cultural resources.

Anti-gang initiatives themselves can create positions for young people to fill. For example, young people who have been deeply involved with gangs for some time could serve the community as 'gang specialists.'

This can be a productive move because gang-affiliated youths are more likely to respect those with real experience of what it is like to be in a gang than take advice from academic experts or authority figures. An ex-gang member is also less likely to be 'played' by a youth.

When an ex-gang member talks about why they joined a gang and what made them decide to leave, their stories and advice will carry more weight because young people can relate more easily to their experiences.

CHAPTER 24: Getting Out of a Gang (Youth's Guide)

This chapter is aimed at young gang members who are considering – either through successful interventions or through their own harsh experiences – how to escape a gang.

Understand that the reality of being in a gang is much worse than the fantasy. There is no happy ending by staying with a gang. I can't promise your new life is going to be easy but there are many people out there who want you to succeed and will support you through the transition.

Here are a few simple steps that can make it that bit easier to get out of a gang:

- ✓ Affirm your power to change. The more you tell yourself that you can and will change direction, the easier you will find it to believe that.
- ✓ Thoughts of failure and low self-belief are a hangover from the past and you can choose to replace these with positive messages.
- ✓ You did not choose the neighbourhood or family you were born in to. You are not the first or last person who will seek a solution for your hurt in a gang.
- ✓ Gangs are a dead-end street and you deserve better than that.

Fill Your Life with Activities

There is a saying that 'the Devil finds work for idle hands.' Anti-social behaviour such as vandalism and fighting are often linked to boredom and many present and former gang members admit that they got into gangs because they didn't have anything else to do.

Now that you are discovering a new self-confidence, it is a good idea to push yourself to join one of the many activities or sports clubs on offer in the community. From football, the gym, arts programmes, drama schools, street dance and film clubs there are usually plenty of opportunities once you get out of the bored mind-set.

You might even consider setting up a club where there is a gap in the market (e.g. a parkour or BMX club). If you are really at a loose end, consider simply spending some quality time with your family or visiting a relative you haven't seen for a while.

Filling your time with activities will make you less available to gang friends who may try and persuade you into coming back, especially if you are having a low moment.

If a gang friend is inspired by what you are doing, consider getting them to join or set up a club with you.

Ditch the Gangster Look

As you grow in confidence you will begin to realise that the gangster clothes, bling, swagger and lingo are all a costume or a mask designed to hide who you really are. People who are really confident don't seek to shock, threaten or demand respect and attention through their appearance. They are 'comfortable in their own skin.'

As you realise you are a good person with the ability to succeed on your own merit, you too will drop the act and feel more able to relax and be yourself.

Dressing down will also help you to stay off the radar of rival gangs if that is worrying you.

Get good at saying no. Some of your previous gang friends won't be ready to make the break and will want to find ways to bring you back into their lives. They may call or text you regularly or track you down in the street to encourage you to hang out with them. If you stop taking calls or responding to texts they should soon get the message.

It is also good to have a stock phrase or two ready to counter any attempts at persuasion. The following group activity will help you to come up with some:

Activities: Disconnecting from the Gang

Try this!

In this simple role play, one person should play the part of an ex-gang member and the others are old friends looking to connect.

Step 1: The gang members should try and persuade the other person to hang out with them. They should try three times.
Step 2: The person then has to go away for five minutes and come up with a response to turn down each of the three attempts.
Step 3: Change roles.

When everyone has had a go at being the ex-gang member, discuss which responses were the most effective and whether it was easier to say no when there was a prepared response ready to use. Use this discussion to mentally store away some stock rejections.

Find new friends. As well as avoiding old friends and gang associates, start building up a new support network. Connect only with people who support and believe in you as they will help reinforce your own affirmations.

Remember, real friends will accept and support you but won't make excuses for you. They will have higher expectations than your former crew and will hold you accountable for your decisions. Ask for support. Once you have made that courageous decision to leave a gang, you will find plenty of support available to you. Community police officers, school response officers, teachers, sports coaches, activity leaders, religious figures and even parents are just some of the people you can talk to if you need some support and encouragement.

A Note on Gang Compliance

In order to operate successfully in society, gangs demand compliance from their members. This compliance may be secured partly through guilt (because you owe them for looking out for you and saving your skin) but often through violence or the threat of violence.

The fear of a beating is often enough to stop any thoughts of leaving a gang. It is important to understand that, while there is a risk of being punished, the threats are often designed as a deterrent rather than a promise.

Despite ideas like 'blood in, blood out,' plenty of people leave a gang without any punishment. The idea of an all-seeing eye, common in many abusive relationships, is an exaggeration that plays on your paranoia.

Once you cut all ties with a gang and embrace your new community, the gang will more than likely move on to target more vulnerable people.

CHAPTER 25: Getting Out of a Gang (Parent's guide)

This chapter is aimed at parents who are worried that their children are at risk of joining or being drawn deeper into a gang. There are a few things that you can do to intervene successfully, but first start by understanding the reasons why young people join gangs. Some of the reasons young people often give for joining gangs include:

- Respect and reputation.
- Acceptance and belonging.
- Material reward.
- Control over people.
- Protection.
- Excitement.

Give your child a reality check. If your child is on the outskirts of a gang, they may be drawn into the illusion of money and power and enjoying the excitement of the gang lifestyle. The voices of the elders may be strong, so your voice will have to be stronger.

Here are some of the realities to remind them of:

- ✓ Being in a gang involves criminal activity.
- ✓ Being arrested, even for minor offences, can make getting a job harder.
- ✓ If you are caught carrying a knife, you will be arrested. The law doesn't

care whether you intended to use it or not.

- ✓ Carrying a knife means that knife is highly likely to be used against them. Ask them to think about how you would feel about losing them.
- ✓ Using a knife can end with another mother losing a child.
- ✓ A gang will demand retaliation. This won't end until someone is killed or seriously hurt.
- ✓ Being in a gang will affect their mental health. They will become paranoid and perhaps suffer from PTSD if they witness something horrible.
- ✓ Being part of a gang, which commits a serious crime could end with a jail sentence under Joint Enterprise laws.
- ✓ Dealing in drugs causes vulnerable people to become ill and sometimes die. The drugs industry is responsible for countless deaths.
- ✓ Stay calm and positive. If your child admits to being in a gang, it is important not to lose your cool as this will drive them away. Instead:
- ✓ Try to understand their reasons for joining.
- ✓ Ask questions but don't accuse.
- ✓ Listen to their answers and try to put yourself in their shoes.
- ✓ Ask what you can do to help.
- ✓ Work with them to find alternatives.
- ✓ Make sure they are aware of the consequences of gang activity.
- ✓ Show them documentaries about gangs.

Make sure you keep communication channels open and are always there for them when they need you.

CHAPTER 26: 2020 Dreams & 2020 Rising: Workshops & Consultation

This resource is a 2020 Dreams publication in partnership with 2020 Rising.

What Is 2020 Rising?

2020 Rising focuses on those difficult topics nobody seems to want to talk about and asks the questions most of us are too scared to ask.

The 2020 Rising programme combines workshops, training programmes, consultations, lectures, life coaching and resources and tackles some of the toughest subjects in the UK today including youth street gangs, gun and knife crime and illegal drugs.

Before we can hope to make positive changes in our communities we need to have our eyes wide open and be prepared to face some stark truths about what is happening on our streets. 2020 Rising is committed to raising real awareness, engaging with all members of afflicted communities and then taking positive action which will actually have a chance of working.

What is 2020 Dreams?

2020 Dreams is our cutting edge programme of workshops for schools and other youth institutions.

2020 Dreams' many specialist workshops are divided into five sections, each covering a specific area of concern to teachers, students, parents and the wider community.

Sex and Relationships Education (SRE)

Our Sex and Relationships Education section covers all aspects of relationships and sexuality as they apply to young people. Workshops are designed to be age appropriate and to work well alongside your existing SRE programmes.

Some of the workshops we run cover the physical changes and social pressures which accompany puberty.

Building awareness and resilience in our young people helps them to navigate this tough area more skilfully.

Workshops include:

- ✓ Puberty Workshop
- ✓ Sexting and Online Privacy
- ✓ Teen Drinking: Alcohol and Sex
- ✓ Pornography Education
- ✓ Sex and Peer Pressure (SAY NO!)

This section also looks at when relationships turn bad and become unhealthy. Our workshops are designed to help protect young people from becoming victims or perpetrators of abuse.

Such workshops include:

- ✓ Teenage Relationship Abuse
- ✓ Sexual Bullying and Inappropriate Behaviours
- ✓ Consent, Rape, Harassment

There are also hard-hitting workshops on the widespread abuse of children and young people in society. For example, we cover:

- Child Sexual Exploitation (CSE)
- Survival Sex
- Forced Marriages
- Female Genital Mutilation (FGM)

We also help young people to make better decisions around their sexual health and life choices. They are particularly useful in areas with a high incidence of teenage pregnancies.

Relevant workshops include:

- Teenage Pregnancy Education
- STD Awareness
- Contraception Awareness
- Sexuality and Making Better Decisions

Life, Crime and Social Survival

Our life, crime and social survival series focuses on a wide range of issues that impact on the lives of our young people every day.

Some apply to children of all ages and in all communities; these include:

- ✓ Peer Pressure
- ✓ Road Safety Awareness
- ✓ Stranger Danger

Others are more likely to affect older children and teenagers although the earlier you can build awareness, the easier it will be to protect our young people. Topics include:

- ✓ Drugs and Alcohol Awareness
- ✓ Addiction (Gaming, Food, Sex, Tattoos, Drugs, etc.)
- ✓ Gun and Knife Crime Awareness
- ✓ Gang Prevention and Awareness

We also have developed a range of courses focusing on issues that are prominent in the news today. These include:

- ✓ Fear of Terrorist Attack
- ✓ Human Trafficking and Modern-Day Slavery
- ✓ Staying Safe Online
- ✓ Radicalisation and Extremism

Other workshops in the series, include:

- Crime and Punishment
- Domestic Violence

We regularly add new workshops to our Sex and Relationships Education and Life, Crime and Social Survival sections. Check our website for the very latest offerings: www.2020dreams.org.uk

Anti-Bullying and Conflict Resolution

Bullying and conflict, within schools, on the streets and now online, is an ever-present factor as young people work to express themselves and negotiate relationships. Our anti-bullying and conflict workshops tackle these issues head on and can focus on general conflict or specific forms of bullying.

Examples include:

- Conflict Resolution
- Islamophobia in Schools
- Cyber Bullying
- Racial Discrimination
- Age Discrimination
- Homophobic Bullying
- Sexual Bullying

We also offer workshops which help young people to understand the roots of conflict and work to develop a more inclusive set of values.

These workshops include:

- Human Rights
- Diversity Activities – Anti-Semitism and Religious Discrimination
- Respect and Tolerance
- Promoting Cultural Awareness
- Gender Equality

Mental, Emotional and Physical Wellbeing

Mental health is a huge topic that is regularly making the news and government debates. 2020 Dreams provide an extensive range of mental health related workshops.

Here are some of the programmes we offer:

- Mental Health and Positive Thinking
- Body Image and Low Self Esteem
- Managing Emotions: Death and Bereavement
- Understanding Depression
- Eating Disorders
- Suicide Workshop
- Self-Harm Workshops
- Anxiety and OCD

We can also provide workshops to help protect children's mental health by developing life skills and the ability to support one another.

Some examples include:

- Healthy Relationships
- Confidence Building
- Healthy Eating
- Personal Hygiene and Grooming
- How to be a Supportive Friend Workshop
- Managing Stress During Exams Workshops

Business, Career and Money Management

We believe every young person, no matter what background he or she comes from, has the potential to succeed in life. What they sometimes lack is the vision and the opportunity.

2020 Dreams Business, Career and Money Management workshops are focused on helping children and teenagers to plan for a future of achievement and success.

Workshops we run include:

- Enterprise Workshops
- Financial Responsibility, Money and Budgeting

All 2020 Dreams workshops and teacher trainings can be provided anywhere in the UK and are run by skilled, experienced, DBS-cleared facilitators.

We use proven techniques such as role play scenarios and open forum-based discussion groups to engage with young people and maximise the benefits they will take away with them.

Our workshops are fully risk-assessed and tailored to the particular age group and demographic of your school or institution. We can also create customised programmes tailored specifically to your needs.

For the latest information on our range of workshops, please visit www.2020dreams.org.uk

References

1. Getting Real with Guns and Knives' Sampson, L, 2018.
2. 'London Gang Crime: 11 young men have been stabbed to death in the capital in 2018 – and its only March!', Get West London, 2018
3. 'Living with Knife Crime: both my sons have been stabbed', Bannock, C. (The Guardian, Beyond the Blade), 2018
4. 'Gangs and Gang Crime: Advice for Parents', www.nidirect.co.uk, 2018
5. 'Knife Crime up 14% Because Gang Warfare is Becoming "Embedded in our Culture"', Walker, P. (The Telegraph), 2017
6. 'Police Data Shows Crime Rising at Increasing Rate in England and Wales', Travis, A. (The Guardian), 2017
7. 'Gangland' (TV Documentary), Channel Five, 2016
8. 'The Handbook of Gangs', Decker, S.H. and Pyrooz, D.C. (Eds), 2015
9. 'The Re-Evolution of American Street Gangs', June, D.L., Khatibloo, M. and Estevane, G. (Eds), 2015
10. 'Changing Course: Preventing Gang Membership', Simon, T.R., Ritter, N.M. and Mahendra, R.R. (eds), 2014
11. 'We Need to Get It Right: A health check into the Council's role in tackling child sexual exploitation', Overview and Scrutiny Committee, Birmingham City Council, 2014
12. 'Gangs 101: Understanding the Culture of Youth Violence', Esperanza, 2010
13. 'Ben killers told rival gang: we stabbed your white boy', Evening Standard, 2009
14. 'Dying to Belong', Centre for Social Justice, 2009
15. 'Gang Prevention: A Resource Guide on Youth & Gangs', Department of

Justice (Canada), 2009
16. 'OJJDP Comprehensive Gang Model: Planning for Implementation', OJJDP, 2009
17. 'Gangs: Awareness, Prevention, Intervention', Glasgow, J.W., 2007
18. 'Youth Gangs and Schools', Centre for Mental Health in Schools, UCLA, 2007
19. 'What Future for Kurt' (TV Documentary), Panorama, 2005
20. 'Risk Behaviours Among Young Mexican-American Gang-associated Females: sexual relations, partying, substance use and crime', Cepeda, A. and Valdez, A., 2003
21. 'Youth Gangs: Problem and Response', Spergel, I., 1993

Printed in Great Britain
by Amazon

68647526R00095